BEAT
the
BLUES

GOD'S
CURE
FOR
DEPRESSION

Beat the Blues

Help in combating
"the common cold of emotional dis-ease."

JOHN   ALLAN   LAVENDER

Tyndale House
Publishers, Inc.
Wheaton, Illinois

First Printing, April 1982
Library of Congress Catalog Card Number 81-84991
ISBN 0-8423-0128-3, paper
Copyright © 1982 by John Allan Lavender
All rights reserved
Printed in the United States of America

Contents

1

GOD LOVES YOU
AND I'M TRYING TO

A mother was having increasing difficulty getting her son
out of bed to go to church. This hadn't always been true.
At one time he had been enthusiastic about church, but
things had begun to change. One Sunday he was
particularly resistant to the idea of going.

She shook him and said, "Son, you've just got to get
up and go to church."

"I don't want to go," he mumbled, and rolled over.

"Give me two reasons why you shouldn't go," she
pleaded.

"Well," he said, "for one thing, a lot of people down
there don't like me. For another, every time I show up
they think of something for me to do, and no matter how
hard I try I never seem to do it right."

"Those are pretty good reasons," she agreed, "but,
son, you just have to get up and go to church."

"I gave you two reasons why I shouldn't have to,"
he replied. "You give me two reasons why I should."

"OK," she said. "First of all—you're thirty-eight years
old. Second—you're the minister!"

I begin in this lighthearted way for two reasons. One,
while depression is a heavy subject, I don't want this book
to be heavy. Hopefully, the humor scattered throughout

will help make a point. At the very least, it will provide
a change of pace. Two, if you understand that even
ministers get depressed, maybe you won't be quite
so shook up if and/or when it happens to you.

THE MANY FACES OF DEPRESSION

Depression has been called the common cold of
emotional dis-ease or psychological pathology. No one is
immune. All of us are victimized from time to time. Like
the common cold, depression is pesky to treat, wears
many faces, and comes in varying degrees of intensity.

For a long time I have thought about writing a book on
this subject. I felt it could help a lot of *other* people!
However, I wondered if I could write such a book with
any degree of integrity and sensitivity, because of my
limited experience with depression.

Back in 1951, I did have a rather severe bout of
depression. Every afternoon around 4 o'clock I would
slip into a deep melancholy. An awful, black mood would
come over me, last several hours, and then mysteriously
lift. It was very unpleasant. This went on for almost two
months. While sitting in a dentist's chair one morning,
I began to get a handle on it. He had made the mistake
of asking how I was and I told him! Between drilling,
hammering, rinsing, packing, air-drying (ouch!), filling,
and billing (!), my dentist friend took advantage of
my inability to talk back and called my attention to
a few things.

I had a new home, a new car, a new job, and a new
baby. I had extended myself financially to build an
addition on our new home. "And"—it was almost a
throwaway line—"you wouldn't be quite normal if, as a
young professional, you weren't tinged with at least a mild
fear of failure."

I spent the rest of the day "working" on that. The more
I thought about it the clearer it became that my fear of

failure wasn't mild, it was deep-seated! I remembered some things I had learned about myself while growing up.

At school I did rather well with short-term commitments. In one-semester courses I usually got an "A" or "B." If a course ran two semesters (or longer), my level of performance fell off.

The same thing was true of various jobs I held to get through school. With great enthusiasm I would make a tremendous start, but boredom would soon set in and my efficiency would go down. When I worked for the *Oakland Tribune* as a distribution manager, I loved to go into a district which was in a state of disarray, put it together, get the routes covered, and the kids all making money. Then I'd lose interest. When they gave me a district of my own, I got it shipshape, earned "Top District of the Month" award, became bored, and the level of my performance tumbled. Part of this was due to lack of discipline. Part to the fact I had not yet found my niche in life. When I got involved in full-time ministry the pattern changed. Or at least it seemed to, until that summer of 1951.

For an evangelist—my sphere of ministry at the time—it is critical to keep booked months ahead. I had become so preoccupied with completing the addition to our new home before I hit the road again, that I had allowed my scheduling for the fall to go by the boards. September was coming on fast and I had several open dates. My reputation, maybe even my career, was on the line. That day, after my stint in the dentist's chair, I realized consciously what had been bugging me subconsciously and making me depressed. "Was this a 'curse' I'd have to live with for life—starting off with a bang, losing interest, and then experiencing declining performance?"

My first year as an evangelist had been tremendous—beyond all expectations. I loved it. The problem wasn't loss of interest. It was a case of misplaced priorities complicated by trying to do too much with too little time and money. The resultant schedule gaps had triggered my deep-rooted fear of failure. Well, I got busy with a capital "B"! The fall schedule was quickly filled and, not so incidentally, I saw to it my bookings were never again left untended. I hit the road. The dark mood lifted and never returned. So, in my mind depression was equated with that deep pit—that tunnel of darkness with no apparent end. How, therefore, could I write a book on depression when my own life, except for that one episode, had been so free of it? I was to learn, however, that depression wears many faces and comes in a variety of degrees.

THE "COMMON COLD" HIT ME

In 1977 I developed a pesky, persistent case of sinusitis which, after eighteen months, gradually wore me down physically and emotionally. At the insistance of one of our elders (and with his assistance, I might add, for the cost was substantial) I went to Scripps Clinic to see if we could get at the root of the problem. Among the symptoms I listed on the intake form was: "Discouragement at not getting better." The receiving doctor said, "I see you are suffering from depression. While we're running these other tests, I'd like you to talk to one of our psychiatrists."

I gulped inwardly and tried to hide my sudden sense of panic. I don't know why the term "psychiatrist" is so scary. The ones I know are rather nice people. So was this fellow. I talked a little bit about my discouragement at having this pesky illness for eighteen months. He was compassionate and understanding, so I grew a bit more courageous. This was costing a bundle. I decided to get my money's worth and shared some other things which were bothering me. At the end of an hour (which literally flew by), he said calmly, "I see you're suffering from mild recurring depression."

That made two of them—the receiving doctor and the psychiatrist! So I began to take seriously what I was hearing. We were paying a lot of money for a diagnosis.

It was foolish not to pay attention to what I was being told. "I want to work on this," I said. And we made an appointment for the following day. That night in my room I gave the matter some deep thought: If this can happen to me, it can happen to anyone. I have a healthy self-image, a fairly happy view of myself and my life, and if I am suffering from "mild recurring depression" it can happen to anyone. Maybe I was more qualified than I realized to write that book on depression. But first of all I had some work to do.

I took three weeks off to rest, read, think, and pray. It was during this period of time I discovered that depression is what some call "the common cold of psychological pathology." We all go through times when we suffer from what we call "the blues," or "discouragement." When it becomes chronic, as it had in my case, the technical term is "mild recurring depression." I began to pray the Lord would show me not only the cause of such depression, but also his cure for it.

SOME BASIC GROUND RULES

In the course of my pilgrimage I learned a lot of things. For instance, depression is far too complex for "easy-answerism." If I appear to offer easy answers in this book, please understand I know depression is a very complex emotional disorder which does not succumb to simple solutions.

Second—and I share this by way of a warning—I learned not to apply everything I heard or read to myself. There's something in us that tends to want to do that. I suppose every college student of Abnormal Psych has the experience of winding up with every symptom of every disease. It must be part of human nature to personalize things. But please, do not apply everything you read about depression in magazines and books—*not even this one*—to yourself.

Another thing worth remembering is that while

depression attacks all of us at some time or other in some form or other, like the common cold it goes away. It doesn't come to stay. One of my most cherished possessions is a silver dollar which was given to me by a former navy frogman who, during World War II, had the task of putting dangerous explosives on the underside of enemy ships. It was a frightening task. To help him deal with fear he carried this silver dollar in his wetsuit where he could feel it from time to time to remind him of a little phrase which appears many times in Scripture and which meant a great deal to him: ". . . it came to pass." Those four words helped him handle the terror of being in a very perilous situation. It was temporary. It "came to pass."

Depression is like that. It doesn't come to stay. It comes to pass. It will go away. Frustration isn't final. Failure isn't final. Moods of despair are not final. Feelings of depression are not final. The sunlight of God's joy will come again.

THREE KINDS OF DEPRESSION AND THEIR CAUSES

The real intellectual in our family is my wife, Lucille. Both of us went to the same university. When *she* graduated, the dean said to the president: "May I present Lucille Lavender, magna cum laude." When I graduated, the dean said to the president, "*John* Lavender? Laudy, how cum!" So Lucille is the one with the brains in our family. I'm not a medical expert or licensed psychotherapist. I am a pastor. However, without sounding erudite or bookish, and while avoiding as much technical jargon as possible, I would like to explain the three kinds of depression medical people recognize.

The first is *endogenous depression*. Its roots are internal and physical. Endogenous depression is caused by a complex chain of biological reactions involving such things as poor diet, atmospheric conditions, hormonal imbalance, inadequate outdoor exercise, hypoglycemia, anemia, lack of vitamins, a "slow leak" of psychic energy due to age or persistent illness, jetlag, other "tinkering" with your body clock and disruptions in the general rhythm of your life.

While most schools of mental health see depression as wearing many faces and springing from many causes, some psychotherapists, notably in Great Britain, hold *all* depression to be endogenous. Other forms of this disorder, they argue, are rooted in the basic cause of *all* depression: imbalance in one's body chemistry.

That may be an oversimplification. However, it is true your moods and physical state are like railroad tracks. When one zigs, the other zigs. When one zags, the other zags. A certain amount of turning, rising, and falling are par for the course. Future research will undoubtedly provide additional understanding of these normal swings or undulations, as well as insight into the extent to which your emotions are affected by your physical state. Suffice it to say: they are! The dark moods which result from internal and physical causes are classified under the general heading of endogenous depression.

A second major form of this disorder is *exogenous depression*. Its roots are external and situational. Normally it has to do with a sense of loss. The loss of a spouse. A child. A parent. A friend. A job. Position. Power. Money. Self-esteem. Sometimes the sense of loss grows out of the widening gap between expectations and reality. It may be rooted in loneliness, or in situations which simply overwhelm you.

The third major classification is neurotic depression. Its roots are internal and attitudinal. *Neurotic depression is the focal point of this book. If you think about it just a bit, you'll realize the one thing over which you have any significant control is your attitude. Thus, by learning to deal with the causes of neurotic depression, you will increase your ability to deal more creatively with exogenous, and even endogenous, depression. If you build a record of successes in one area, you can carry that record into other areas. For instance, a positive mental attitude can have a healthy effect on your body chemistry and help you cope with endogenous depression.*

This book is an invitation to think and share with me—to try to identify the wrong attitudes which perhaps you don't even recognize at the moment, but which Satan is cleverly using to head you into that tunnel which seems to have no end. I encourage you to read, reread— memorize if possible, and internalize Christ's prescription for happiness in the here and now: Matthew 5:3-12. In that way you will not only get hold of the hope and healing God wants you to have but also the *joy* which awaits you.

S. H. Hadley was a missioner like my father. He operated a rescue mission in the Bowery of New York City called the Water Street Mission. One of the "regular customers," as dad used to refer to them, was a fellow called "Major." He came to the mission almost daily, took everything the mission had to give, and then went back to living in the gutter. It went on like that for months.

One night, when S. H. Hadley was particularly weary from a long day, Major came in and asked for money, claiming he needed food and a place to sleep. Hadley came unglued. "I've had it with you, Major! You've been coming in here for months. I've tried to minister to you, tried to encourage you, tried to help you find your way, and it doesn't do any good. Get out of here! I'm not giving you anything anymore!"

Somewhat shocked at this outburst, Major wheeled around and staggered into the night. Hadley went home, climbed into a warm, clean bed and tried to sleep, but couldn't. Finally, about one o'clock in the morning he slipped out of bed, got dressed, and went down to the Bowery. He started going through the flophouses looking for Major. About the fourth or fifth stop, on a floor under a filthy old blanket, he found Major sleeping off a drunk. Somehow he had managed to secure enough money to buy a cheap bottle of wine.

Hadley shook him into consciousness and said, "God loves you and I'm trying to. Come on, get up, and I'll take you back to the mission, fix you something to eat, and give you a clean bed to sleep in." Major shook his head a couple of times and said, "What did you say?"

"I said, 'Come on, get up, and I'll take you back to the mission, fix you something to eat, and give you a clean bed to sleep in.'"

"No, no! What did you say before that?"

"Oh, I said, 'God loves you and I'm trying to.'"

Those seven words pierced through the alcoholic haze in Major's mind. He got up, squared his shoulders, and said, "Really? Are you really trying to love me?"

"Yes, Major, I really am." S. H. Hadley took him back to the mission, and before the night was over Major had found the Savior and in him a new life, a new beginning.

The whole point of this book is that I think God wants you to be able to look in your mirror and say: "God loves you and I'm trying to." There may be many things in you which discourage you from doing so. Things which leave you feeling less than you really are. Things which make you dislike what you see in the mirror. But the good news of the gospel—and the hope I want to give you—is that a day can come when you will look in your mirror and not only say "God loves you and I'm trying to," but "God loves you *and I do, too!*" When you reach that point, you will have entered into the joy of the Lord—the joy Jesus came to give.

2

WHAT GOD TAUGHT ME
ABOUT NEUROTIC DEPRESSION

Having identified my dis-ease as being neurotic in nature, I asked the Lord to teach me both the cause and cure of my depression. I was led to the Beatitudes. I spent a great deal of time meditating upon them. As I got into the language of the Scripture as originally written, I discovered the word *makarios,* translated "blessed" in most English texts, actually means "happy." "Blithesome." "Joyous." "Spiritually prosperous." "To be envied."[1] In essence Jesus said: Happy, joyous, to be envied are people who develop these positive attitudes.

As I looked at the Beatitudes I asked, "Lord, if this is your prescription for joy, wouldn't a set of anti-attitudes be a surefire formula for depression? Show me what they are and where they come from."

A few hours fell open to me during which I was able to think exclusively about the question I had asked the Lord and, more importantly, to listen to his answer! I believe what you're about to read is from him. It's presented first in outline form, then as an overview to help you begin to let the healing of Christ come to you immediately. Finally, in succeeding chapters you will have a chance to examine each anti-attitude and Christ's correctives in detail, so you, too, can win over neurotic depression.

CHRIST'S BEATITUDES
AND SATAN'S ANTI-ATTITUDES

If, among other things, the Beatitudes are Christ's
prescription for joy (as I believe they are), it follows that
those thoughts and feelings which are antithetical to these
"blessed attitudes" could only come initially from one
source: Satan. The archenemy of God and God's
people. The one whom Jesus described as a thief and liar
(John 10:10; John 4:44).

"What would Satan most want to steal?" I asked God.
The answer came through loud and clear: "Your joy!"
"How does he do it, Father?"
"By lying to you. By distorting what my Son said to
you. By subtly suggesting goals and methods which, if
pursued, will put you in the pit of depression."
"What *are* his distortions, Lord?"

In rapid succession eight words rolled across the
marquee of my mind as if it were one of those moving
signs in Time's Square: perfectionism . . . worthlessness
. . . acquisitiveness . . . hedonism . . . defensiveness . . .
fragmentation . . . aggression . . . depression.

I grabbed a notepad and quickly wrote them down.
Turning to Matthew 5:3-10, I thoughtfully compared them
with what Jesus said. Clearly they were the exact
opposite. Could these be the anti-attitudes which were
a surefire formula for neurotic depression?

I took a clean sheet of paper, folded it lengthwise,
spread it open again and on the left side of the page
wrote out what Jesus said in the Beatitudes as
paraphrased by J. B. Phillips. On the right side of the
page, directly opposite each Beatitude, I wrote one of the
eight words which had flashed across my mind during my
conversation with the heavenly Father. What I saw
astounded me. As I reflected upon the two columns—
contrasting both their meaning and sequence—I was
convinced God had answered my prayer. He had taught
me something about neurotic depression which was both
biblically and psychologically sound.

I added headings to each half page and here's how it looked:

What Jesus Said:	*What Satan Says:*
"How happy are those who know their need for God, for the kingdom of Heaven is theirs!" (Matt 5:3)	Perfectionism
"How happy are those who know what sorrow means, for they will be given courage and comfort!" (Matt. 5:4)	Worthlessness
"Happy are those who claim nothing, for the whole earth will belong to them!" (Matt. 5:5)	Acquisitiveness
"Happy are those who are hungry and thirsty for true goodness, for they will be fully satisfied!" (Matt. 5:6)	Hedonism
"Happy are the merciful, for they will have mercy shown to them!" (Matt. 5:7)	Defensiveness
"Happy are the utterly sincere, for they will see God!" (Matt. 5:8)	Fragmentation
"Happy are those who make peace, for they will be known as sons of God!" (Matt. 5:9)	Aggression

"Happy are those who have
suffered persecution for the
cause of goodness, for the
kingdom of Heaven is
theirs!" (Matt. 5:10)

Depression

I continued to ponder what God was teaching me, and
weeks later several graphics came to mind. One was a
stairway. Depending on how it was approached, it
ascended into joy or decended into depression. Since I
was still in the diagnostic stage of my learning experience,
I assigned one of the eight anti-attitudes to each step—
adding random thoughts as I gained further insight.

PERFECTIONISM

Jesus said: "How happy are those who know their
need for God. . ." (Matt. 5:3). The opposite of this type
of humility is pride. But the manifestation of pride Satan
uses—because he almost never comes to you without a
disguise—is perfectionism. The insidious notion you must
not only be OK, but more than OK. Not only normal and
human, but supernormal, superhuman. The moment
you buy Satan's lie you deny your basic humanity and
position yourself for inevitable failure. From that point
on there is no way you can feel good about yourself.
Every time you even come close to this impossible goal,
you neurotically raise the ante. As a consequence, it's
impossible to ever be satisfied with yourself.

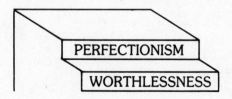

PERFECTIONISM
WORTHLESSNESS

Jesus said: "How happy are those who know what sorrow means. . ." (Matt. 5:4). The opposite of true sorrow for sin is a feeling of utter and complete worthlessness: *"I am absolutely no good!"* Having failed to measure up to the unrealistic demands of perfectionism, you fall prey to chronic regret. On the surface this looks and feels like humility. Actually it is inverted pride, as one part of you looks down on the rest of you and condemns what it sees. You are saddled with a powerful, intimidating sense of unworthiness—what transactional analysis calls "the parent"—in the form of unresolved feelings of failure and guilt.

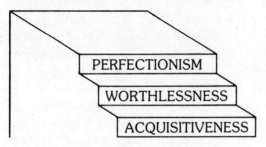

Jesus said: "Happy are those who claim nothing. . ." (Matt. 5:5). Satan's anti-attitude is acquisitiveness. In an attempt to assuage your feelings of worthlessness, you engage in a frantic effort to acquire all the obvious evidences that you are not worthless: success . . . fame . . . power . . . position . . . possessions. There is a saying: "Money won't make you happy, but it certainly makes being unhappy a lot more bearable." The same might be said of acquisitiveness. Achievements of one kind or another definitely do build a sense of self-esteem. Unfortunately, they also have the net effect of triggering additional outbursts of neurotic behavior in the perfectionist because each new "acquisition" must be bigger and better than the last. Hence your feelings of worth are even more firmly *and detrimentally* linked to what you do rather than what you are.

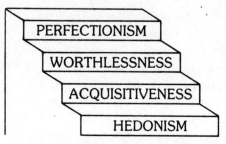

Jesus said: "Happy are those who are hungry and thirsty for true goodness. . ." (Matt. 5:6). Satan's anti-attitude is hedonism. Pleasure is a legitimate part of a normal Christian life. It allows "the child" in you to come out. But ungodliness—hedonism in its uglier forms—is only pleasurable "for a season" (Heb. 11:25, KJV). It soon deteriorates into a jaundiced, jaded view of morality and ethics in which "anything goes." As a result of actions which are self-destructive, you are not only dissatisfied, you are *more and more* dissatisfied. And there is a growing feeling of dread inside: "If none of this satisfies, what on earth will!" Furthermore, Satan has maneuvered you into a position where you are really vulnerable to exogenous depression, because you are resting your whole sense of worth on things which are highly susceptible to loss.

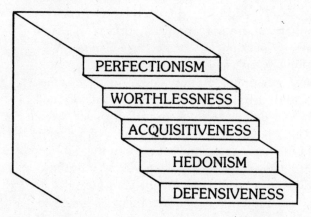

Jesus said: "Happy are the merciful. . ." (Matt. 5:7). The opposite of being kind and forgiving is Satan's anti-attitude: defensiveness. By now you are very much into looking after number one. "If I don't look after me, who will!" You become intolerant, critical, and defensive. Aggression is increasingly apparent. Acts of charity are largely manipulative, designed to get "strokes" for number one. Retroflexed anger is growing, and requires a considerable expenditure of nervous energy to keep it from "showing." Fatigue and deepening depression are inevitable.

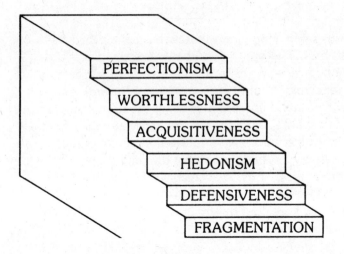

Jesus said: "Happy are the utterly sincere. . ." (Matt. 5:8). The enemy's anti-attitude is fragmentation, expressed in grudging discontent. Out of touch with your true feelings, divided within yourself, lacking the desire or ability to be in touch with the feelings of others, you become a taker. You are also less able and/or willing to accept responsibility for yourself and what you are becoming.

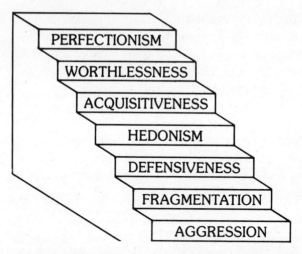

PERFECTIONISM

WORTHLESSNESS

ACQUISITIVENESS

HEDONISM

DEFENSIVENESS

FRAGMENTATION

AGGRESSION

Jesus said: "Happy are those who make peace . . ."
(Matt. 5:9). The opposite of that is hostile aggression.
Many people may not be aware of your anger, because
you retroflex it (that is, turn your anger inward). But *you*
know that inside you are a seething cauldron of rage. You
are almost always angry. You are angry at yourself. At
others. At the world. At God! Restless, driven, and
compulsive, you have become a dripping source of
contentiousness and unrest everywhere you go. As
might be expected, you feel more and more isolated,
because you are shut out by those who are the objects
of your aggression.

Jesus said: "Happy are those who have suffered persecution for the cause of goodness. . ." (Matt. 5:10). The
opposite of that, of course, is an inability to suffer and
benefit from it. Hence, you experience depression
in some form: mild, recurring or more severe. Virtually
out of touch with reality, darkly suspicious and depressed,
you experience temporary moments of release, then bam!
back into the pit. You have fallen prey to the end product
of the anti-attitudes Satan has devised to make you
miserable.

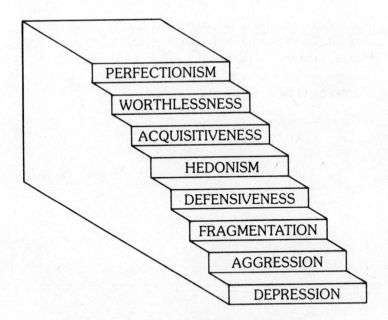

GOD'S CURE FOR DEPRESSION

Lest this sound too "organized" and simplistic, let me hasten to say it is neither necessary nor probable that you will go through all eight steps on each occasion of depression.

You may go directly from perfectionism to worthlessness to depression. Or, from perfectionism to defensiveness to depression. The variables are numerous.

What I have attempted to make clear, however, is that the anti-attitudes spelled out in this chapter are the work of Satan. They are his design to neutralize you—to turn you in upon yourself—to get you so preoccupied with *you* you are no earthly good to yourself, to God, or to anybody else!

The Beatitudes are "wisdom from above" (Jas. 3:17). They are designed to counter the work of Satan and, when followed faithfully, will lead you into joy.

The Beatitudes are not a set of human laws, nor are they a collection of moralisms or pleasant platitudes.

They are a description of Christian character. They are also Christ's explanation of how life works out best. Hence, they may accurately be called: God's cure for depression. Let's look at them one by one and see how healing can come.

3

IT'S OK TO BE HUMAN

How happy are those who know their need for God, for the kingdom of Heaven is theirs! Matthew 5: 3

Rx for   PERFECTIONISM

An abundant, satisfying, joyful life! That's what you want, isn't it? Well, if Jesus has *his* way, that's what you'll have. He made that clear in a declaration recorded in the Gospel of John. He was describing how you can experience God's best in your life. In the midst of some heavy teaching Jesus paused for a moment to give this exciting explanation: "These things I have spoken to you, that My joy may be in you, and that your joy may be made full" (John 15:11, NASB). It is Jesus' desire that you live an abundant, satisfying, joyful life!

On the other hand, as demonstrated in the preceding chapters, Satan's desire for you is the exact opposite. For every Beatitude Jesus gave as a prescription for happiness, the adversary has devised an anti-attitude which, if not dealt with quickly, courageously, and creatively, will send you sliding into neurotic depression.

This means that neurotic depression—which I defined as being internal and attitudinal—is not just a disorder. It is also a symptom. Among other things it is symptomatic of the fact that, for the moment at least, you have forgotten your essential humanity. Having believed the Great Deception—that you should be *more* than human—you feel driven to be right and do right in everything all the time. You have fallen prey to what many feel is the primary cause of neurotic depression: perfectionism.

THE MEANING OF BEING PERFECT

But didn't Jesus tell us to be perfect? Yes, he did. Matthew 5:48 says exactly that: "Therefore you are to be perfect, as your heavenly Father is perfect" (NASB). What you need to remember, however, is that being perfect and perfectionism are not the same thing.

Matthew 5:48 is an excellent illustration of the unfortunate limitations of language when we attempt what I call a one-on-one, or word-for-word, translation from Greek to English.

In the Sermon on the Mount (Matt. 5—7) Jesus is talking about Christian character—how you are to live and love. The word translated "perfect" (5:48) comes from the root word *telos,* which means target. Goal. The point at which you aim. As used in this particular verse, it means to be complete or to enter into completeness.

Jesus is saying: In terms of character—in the quality of your life and love—let it be your aim to grow up. To come of age. To be mature. "Be perfect" is his invitation and exhortation to become whole—to have as your aim the goal of being truly human, of becoming all God meant you to be when he made you in his image (Gen. 1:26). That's a far cry from perfectionism!

Perfectionism isn't being truly human. It's the neurotic demand that you be more than human.

Perfectionism isn't being truly normal. It's the neurotic requirement that you be supernormal.

Perfectionism isn't being OK. It's neurotic insistance that you be more than OK.

It's the same old trick Satan used on Adam and Eve when he said to them, "If you eat of that tree, you won't die. You'll be superhuman. You'll be gods!" (Gen. 3:4, 5, author's paraphrase.) The moment Adam and Eve bought that deception, they lost their essential humanity.
They became victims of perfectionism. Their goals and expectations were unrealistic. Unattainable. *Inhuman!*

Perhaps you're being victimized by the same illusion. If so, Jesus wants you to know it's OK to be human. Why? Because that's what you are!

When God made you, he made you a human, not a god. In the Beatitudes Jesus is saying, I want to help you and show you how to be *truly* human. How to be whole. How to be complete. How to be the person God meant you to be. And, as I've said, that's a far cry from perfectionism.

PERFECTIONISM DEFINED

Perfectionism is not an honest commitment to excellence.

Perfectionism is not the warm, good feeling of deep satisfaction you get from a job well done.

Perfectionism is not an earnest desire to measure up to your full potential in some area of special competence.

All of these are healthy, human, and good. They are character traits you should cherish and aim toward.

But perfectionism, whether caught or taught, is a compulsive obsession which drives you toward totally unattainable goals. *Perfectionism insists you be right and do right in everything all the time.*

Perfectionism demands that you maintain a slavish sensitivity to do's and don'ts. To shoulds and should nots. To oughts and ought nots.

Perfectionism saddles you with exaggerated concerns

for such things as being on time—all the time! Doing the right thing—all the time! Fulfilling each and every demand, *not of Jesus,* but of a nagging inner voice which insists that at all times and in all situations you be totally responsible and dependable, even if it kills you. And sometimes it does, if not physically, perhaps emotionally. You grow weary—not in well doing, but in not doing well, in not being able to reach the unreachable star of perfection.

The kindest thing you can do for yourself right now is lower your expectations. Give youself permission to be imperfect. Without surrendering a healthy commitment to excellence in some area of special competence, learn to live within your limitations.

The telephone rang in a bank. It was after hours. The only one on duty was the janitor. He picked up the phone and said, "Hello."

A rather excited, harassed voice on the other end of the phone said, "I want to know what the federal reserve discount rate is. What the prime paper rate is. If all this foreign travel will upset our currency and what escalating energy costs are doing to the dollar." The janitor thought for a moment and then answered, "Mister, I told you all I know about banking when I said, 'hello.'"

Praise God for people who have a healthy awareness of their limitations and are prepared to live within them. They make it easier for the rest of us to do the same.

PERFECTIONISM AND PEOPLE-PLEASING

A moment ago I suggested it's hard to tell whether perfectionism is caught or taught. The possibility it *may* be taught should lead parents, teachers, and other authority figures to shift the focus of effort from trying to make children good to helping children be whole.

Let me repeat that: *Parents, teachers and other authority figures need to shift the focus of effort*

*from trying to make children good to helping children
be whole.*

Matthew 20 illustrates why. The mother of the sons
of Zebedee came to Jesus with a request. "Command that
in Your kingdom these two sons of mine may sit, one on
Your right and one on Your left" (Matt. 20:21, NASB).
Without realizing it, perhaps, this mother was trying to
make her sons into something they weren't meant to be.
She was saddling them with totally unattainable expectations because, as Jesus explained (Matt. 20:23),
the seating order in heaven is something God alone
will decide.

The devastating effect of perfectionistic demands is
further revealed when we're told, "and hearing this
[the discussion between Jesus and an overly ambitious
mother], the ten became indignant at the two brothers"
(20:24). Her motherly insistence that her boys be more
than they were meant to be not only hurt them, it also
angered their fellows. It not only put pressure on them,
it also strained their relationships.

Perfectionism is tough enough to deal with when it's
internal. It becomes even rougher if people of importance
to you—parents, siblings, your mate, pastors, those you
work with and for, friends, etc.—project their perfectionism onto you. A snowball effect follows. That which
is external feeds that which is internal. As the ante
goes up your self-esteem goes down, sometimes to a
dangerous level.

A lad went to see a doctor. "Are you in pain, Sonny?"
the doctor asked. "No, sir," the youngster replied,
"the pain is in me." A haunting way of saying inordinate
concern for high achievement in order to receive acceptance, approval, and affection can be a pain—a deep
pain. It is one from which some people never recover.

Dr. Roger Barrett, a fine Christian psychologist,
professor, and head of the psychology department at
Malone College, tells about a fifteen-year-old girl, a high

school sophomore, who, after maintaining a straight "A" average received her first "B." She committed suicide, leaving a note which succinctly portrayed the peril of perfectionism: "If I fail in what I do, I fail in what I am."[1] The monster of perfectionism can be brutal, and we must slay this demon in Jesus' name!

Dr. Bernard L. Ramm, a prestigious evangelical scholar, writes, "The perfectionist is a person who is threatened by life. He has a deep-seated anxiety about the whole business of living. Accordingly, part of his strategy is to highly systematize life. He structures everything according to a rigid pattern. Only by living within that pattern can he feel secure.

"But he does not stop there. He makes imperious demands upon others to conform to this rigid pattern. . . . if a perfectionist becomes a Christian, he is apt to put himself under the most rigid spiritual discipline. This may come out as hours of prayer, or hours of Bible study, or perfect attendance at church meetings. It also issues in a neat system of do's and don'ts which become the barometer of spirituality. The halo fits very tightly."[2]

PERFECTIONISM AND CONDITIONAL LOVE

Most perfectionists are people who lost their childhood. In an effort to meet expectations coupled with approval and acceptance, they grew up prematurely. In most cases they were raised in homes where they received conditional love. They were loved—or only *felt* loved—if they measured up to the expectations of their parents.

What a contrast from the day they were born. As infants were they ushered into a home where mother and father loved them because they were good? Because they did the right things? Because they measured up to all expectations? Of course not. They were loved for themselves!

But somewhere along the line that little one began to

learn a painful lesson: to feel loved it was not enough to *be* something, it was necessary to *do* something. The child had to compare favorably with—perhaps even exceed—the performance of others. With that discovery one of two things happened—the child moved toward becoming a perfectionist, or, equally sad, he or she quit altogether and settled for mediocrity.

Someone has said happiness is the stopping place between too little and too much. It seems to me that somewhere between utter indifference to excellence on one hand and inordinate concern for high achievement *as the price of approval* on the other, is the middle ground on which parents should stand. Here they can provide their children with a healthy, loving support system which frees them to grow into wholeness without becoming victimized by perfectionism.

One set of parents I know did it this way. They encouraged excellence in their children. They made themselves available to help if asked. When major examinations or times of testing came, they reminded their children, "You've worked hard. You've studied diligently. We're going to pray you'll relax and let what your head knows flow through your hand onto the examination paper. But remember—win, lose, or draw—we love you." That's healthy. It's human. And it frees kids to grow without being victimized by perfectionism.

HOW TO GET RID OF PERFECTIONISM

If your goal is to be truly human, where do you begin? The question reminds me of a chap who went to see a psychiatrist. He was wearing a jacket with one orange sleeve and one green sleeve. His trousers had one purple leg and one yellow leg. A necklace of carrots hung around his neck and a parrot sat on his head. "What can I do for you?" the psychiatrist asked. And the parrot replied, "How can I get this thing off my feet?"

Jesus explained how to get rid of the monstrosity called perfectionism when he said: "Blessed are the poor in spirit, for theirs is the kingdom of heaven" (Matt. 5:3, NASB).

As part of God's cure for depression, let me suggest a paraphrase:

RX *for perfectionism: Happy are the truly human—those who are free to experience all their feelings, accept their imperfections, and give themselves permission to grow. God's will—their highest good—will come to them in the now.*

BECOME TRULY HUMAN

As I see it, Jesus is saying the first principle you must follow in defeating neurotic depression is to become truly human. You are more than a body. Therefore, your spirit must be right. The key word in Matthew 5:3 is "spirit."

What does it mean to be poor in spirit? Not to go around like a whipped puppy dog! Rather, it means learning to see yourself as God sees you. It means accepting your essential humanity.

One of the most encouraging verses in all of Scripture is one which reads: "For He Himself [God] knows our frame; He is mindful that we are but dust" (Psa. 103:14).

To be poor in spirit is to recognize your "dustness"—to realize that like dust you are easily blown about by the winds of influence which play upon you.

To be poor in spirit is to see yourself as God sees you—to admit that without his help you're licked.

To be poor in spirit is not to boast of your own goodness, but to acknowledge within you those same capacities which have brought others down.

To be poor in spirit is not to be impressed with yourself, but to be staggered at the fact that God has often protected you from yourself.

To be poor in spirit is not to despise yourself, or elevate yourself, but to know all you have and are is a gift from God.

GET IN TOUCH WITH REALITY

Having lost contact with his essential humanity, the perfectionist is out of touch with reality in the deepest sense of the word. The one who is poor in spirit has gotten back—or is getting back—in touch with the joyous reality of what it means to be truly human. As a consequence, he is free to experience all his feelings.

He lives somewhere between "oh, what a worm am I," which denies the image of God in him, and "oh, what a good boy am I," which denies the power of God at work in him.

He is able to say, "I am not good or bad; I am both good and bad. I am not weak or strong; I am both weak and strong. I am not foolish or wise; I am both foolish and wise. I am not lustful or loving; I am both lustful and loving. In other words I am human. I am a confusing, bewildering, often self-defeating conglomeration of moods and emotions, thoughts and desires, strengths and weaknesses."

Perhaps you're old enough to remember hobos— fellows who went from place to place looking for a handout. One such chap passed a resort area where each cabin bore a different name.

In typical hobo fashion he approached a cabin named "George and the Dragon." When the lady of the house answered his knock on the door and learned what he wanted, she told him in unceremonial terms what she thought of no-good bums and slammed the door in his face. After a moment he rapped gently on the door. When she flung it open, the hobo said, "Excuse me, ma'am, may I speak to George?"

It's like that, isn't it? We have a "George" in us, a

person of rational moods and responses. We also have a "dragon" in us, a person of irrational moods and responses. The one who is truly human is free to experience all these feelings, to accept his imperfections and, at the same time, to give himself permission to grow. You see, it is because, and just because, you are a "George" and a "dragon"—that is, totally human—that you must give that humanity totally to Jesus. If you don't you will live forever in the seventh chapter of Romans— doing the things you don't want to do and not doing the things you do want to do—never experiencing what it means to be more than a conqueror in Christ (Rom. 8:37).

ESTABLISH A BASE LINE

Another way to get in touch with reality is to establish a base line indicating where you see yourself at this moment. Then, accept the fact that God accepts your base line as OK. You see, ". . . God demonstrates His own love toward us, in that while we were yet sinners, Christ died for us" (Rom. 5:8, NASB). It wasn't while you were perfect. It wasn't while you were his friend. It wasn't while you were doing everything he would desire for your good. It was while you were a sinner that Christ died for you.

So establish a base line and accept the fact God says your base line is OK. It's where you are at this moment, and God agrees to meet you there. By doing this you expose your potential for growth. Together, you and God can agree upon a rate of growth which is pleasing to him and possible for you. This will keep you from being caught in a vicious upward spiral of ever-increasing perfectionistic demands which will ultimately exhaust you and plummet you into depression.

Below you will see a "Personal Spiritual Growtho-meter." With pencil in hand let me lead you through

a gentle mental exercise designed to deliver you
from perfectionism and free you to grow.

Personal
Spiritual
Growthometer

10 ——————
9   I am at this point (   ) in my personal
8   spiritual growth, _____!
7
6   I hereby give myself permission to
5   grow from where I am to where God
4   wants me to be.
3   Name _____
2
1   Date _____
0

You will notice a scale starting from 0 to 10. I want you
to establish a base line by indicating on the scale where
you feel you are in the spiritual growth process *as of
today*. (Note: You can't be a zero, because "God don't
make no junk." And you won't be a 10, because that's
not possible in this life. If you feel you ought to be a 10,
when you're only a 3.5, you really do not give yourself
any room to grow. The point is: God accepts you where
you are.)

So find your base line—wherever it is—and indicate
that on the Growthometer.

In the sentence to the right you'll see a pair of
parentheses (   ). Within them write a number corre-
sponding to the level at which you placed yourself on the

Growthometer. For example: "I am at this point (3.5) in my personal spiritual growth." Your number may be higher or lower. Now finish the sentence by adding the words: *"and God says that's OK!"* If you want a biblical basis for it, add the reference: Romans 5:8.

Reflect on the graph for a moment. You are not perfect—you are not a 10. You are not worthless—you are not a 0. Because you have established your base line, you can clearly see you have room to grow. So—on the left side parallel to the Growthometer—between your base line and the figure "10," I want you to write these words: *"My growth potential."* Now then, commit yourself to grow by signing and dating this "permission slip" on the lower right of the Growthometer. Having done so, take note of the fact that as you move along you'll be perfect in God's sight at every point of the growth process!

Hannah Whitall Smith illustrates this tremendous and liberating truth in her book, *The Christian's Secret of a Happy Life.* She refers to apples growing on a tree.[3] They begin as buds, become nodules on a limb, then little hard balls about the size of your smallest fingernail. They continue to mature, growing larger and larger, until ultimately they become luscious, ripe, red apples. The point? At every stage of the growth process they are perfect for *that* point in the process!

So establish a base line and give yourself what God has already given you—permission to grow! You are not only OK for now, you will be OK at each stage of the growth process yet to come!

GOD'S BEST FOR YOU—NOW

Believe me, some exciting things will happen. Matthew 5:3 explains one of them. "Blessed are the poor in spirit, *for theirs is the kingdom of heaven"* (NASB). What on earth is the kingdom of heaven? Jesus defined it for you in his model prayer (Matt. 6:10).

In Hebrew literature there is a style of writing called parallelism. It is found in several forms, one of which is synthetic parallelism. That is, the same thing is said in two different ways. In Matthew 6:10 it works like this: "Thy kingdom come"—first part of the parallelism—"thy will be done, on earth as it is in heaven"—second part of the parallelism. Jesus defined the kingdom of God very simply. The kingdom of God is the will of God lived out in your life now—here on earth—as it is being done in heaven.

In my paraphrase I said, "God's will—their highest good—will come to them in the now." Personalize that. "*My* highest good will come to *me* in the now." God is not a cosmic bellhop who leaps into action at your beck and call. But God is one who has bound himself voluntarily to certain spiritual principles. One of those principles is this: God always gives his best to the truly human. His best is his kingdom—his will here and now.

If you don't believe that, or if you're still shaky on it, think about this: "For the kingdom of God is not eating and drinking, but righteousness (we'll get into that in chapter six) and peace and *joy* in the Holy Spirit. For he who in this way serves Christ is acceptable to God . . ." (Rom. 14:17, 18a).

And think about this! In I Timothy 1:11 Paul speaks of "the glorious gospel of the blessed God." The word translated "blessed" in 1 Timothy 1:11 is the same word Jesus used in Matthew 5:3, "blessed are the poor in spirit." It is the word *makarios* and means happy. Paul is saying, I rejoice in being able to share with you the glorious gospel of our happy God. Now that's fantastic! Your God is a happy God!

It occurs to me as I write that for several years we've been teaching our congregation various attributes of God, yet never once did it occur to us to tell them he is happy. Paul is saying "we have a happy God." And the kingdom of God—the will of God here and now—is learning to

enjoy and experience all the glorious things your happy
God has planned for you.

Suppose your son or daughter came and said, "Mom,
Dad, tomorrow I want to know and do your will all day
long." What would you do? I think I know what I'd do.
I'd sit myself down and make a list of the most wonderful,
delightful, satisfying, challenging, fulfilling experiences
I could think of.

I might include some things my son or daughter would
not include, because, from my perspective as father, I see
good in these activities which youth cannot yet see. But
one thing is certain. If one of my children came to me
and said, "Dad, I want to know and do your will all day
long," I'd do my best to make it the most exciting,
satisfying, joy-filled day of their life. Wouldn't you?

That's what your happy heavenly Father does! God's
will is your highest good. It represents his best. The
moment you become humble-minded, that is, truly
human, you begin to experience God's purpose for your
life in the now. As a consequence, you are spared from a
dual danger which can cause depression: (1) The peril of
achieving an inadequate goal and finding it to be sadly
unfulfilling. (2) The frenzy and fatigue of captivity to
unrealistic goals, that is, perfectionism.

SOMETHING WORTH LIVING FOR

In other words, you are free to be truly human. To be
what God meant you to be all along. God says that's OK.
And to prove it he gives you something worth living for.
A lifelong goal which is not only challenging and exciting,
but manageable and attainable. It is his will—your highest
good—in the now.

Dr. M. Roberts Grover, Jr., is Director of Medical
Education at the University of Oregon Medical School.
I was privileged to hear him give a dynamic lecture on
stress to a group of medical students. Dr. Grover said

many helpful things that day. Among those I wrote down was this: "A first step in lowering stress before it leads to depression is to develop the courage to be imperfect, to admit your humanness." He was talking to a group of young medical students—future doctors who some day might have difficulty living with their imperfections and humanness. His advice: "Develop the courage to be imperfect. Admit your humanness. Then develop a program to progressively approximate a reasonable standard."[4]

That, of course, is what the Beatitudes provide: a reasonable standard. One which is attainable, manageable, and which produces wholeness.

A little boy put it ever so simply in a letter written to God. "Dear God: I'm taking violin, but you shouldn't listen yet, 'cause I still squeak a lot! Love, Russell."

Why not write something equivalent to that little boy's letter to God? Allow yourself to be truly human. Experience all your feelings. Accept your imperfections. Give yourself permission to grow. Start looking forward to the time when you will no longer "squeak a lot." If you do, God's will—your highest good, *the best your happy God can plan*—will come to you in the now.

GUILTY, BUT FORGIVEN—PTL!

How happy are those who know what sorrow means, for they will be given courage and comfort! Matthew 5:4

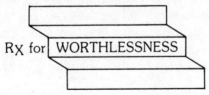

Rx for WORTHLESSNESS

Happy, joyous, growing Christians aren't perfect people! They are people who, while they aren't perfect, also know God loves and accepts them the way they are. This awareness frees them to love and accept themselves. It releases them from the shackles of perfectionism—Satan's counterfeit of true humility—and gives them a handle on depression, while allowing them to begin to experience the joy of the Lord.

A friend heard about the gentle, mental exercise described in chapter three. After trying it she dropped me the following note: "Thanks for sharing the reassuring truth 'it's OK to be human.' I'm guilty of setting such high goals for myself that I find myself in mild depression, having never had a ghost of a chance to live up to those goals. In fact, I find in some areas I often just wallow in the depression without even trying to reach the goal. I see it's impossible to begin with—so why try!

"Many of the goals are not what God would have for me anyway, only ones I 'feel' he has for me, or those I feel others expect of me.

"There's a great measure of peace in being reminded once again that God loves me just as much at my 1.5 level as he will when I reach a lofty 2.3!"

Knowing her well and having rejoiced in her spiritual growth over the years, I could see a smile spill spontaneously across her face and almost hear her laughter as she typed out the reference to "a lofty 2.3!"

Her letter confirmed two things. She really knows the loving, happy God of the New Testament. John 3:16 makes it clear God is loving. First Timothy 1:11 adds the delightful news God is happy. And, as someone has observed, only those who are sure of their loving, happy God have the ability to laugh in his presence.

She also gave evidence of being in touch with what it means to be truly human. She is learning to experience all her feelings, accept her imperfections, and give herself permission to grow.

I hope these two things are happening to you, too. It's impossible to grasp the full significance of Christ's second Beatitude—"Blessed are those who mourn, for they shall be comforted"—without knowing God *as he is* and having come to terms—at least in part—with what it means to be truly human.

NOT PERFECT—JUST FORGIVEN

To be truly human means there is the possibility, or better yet, the probability you'll blow it sometimes. You'll be imperfect. You'll make mistakes. Perish the thought— you'll sin!

There is an erroneous idea wandering around in the minds of not just a few folk today that Christians never sin—that just because we've been born again we will never fail again. Nothing could be further from the truth either biblically or experientially. Anyone who has really read the Scriptures and experienced the Christian life knows it's impossible to be perfect.

I was driving down our main street the other day and saw a bumper sticker: "Christians aren't perfect, just forgiven." I thought to myself, "Hallelujah! We're finally getting the message out. Folks are beginning to understand what it's really like to walk with Jesus."

A chap came into my office wearing a large red and white button with the letters P B P G I F W M Y! "What on earth does that mean?" I asked. With a twinkle in his eyes he responded, "Please be patient, God isn't finished with me yet!"

That's the real truth about the Christian life. When you are truly human—are free to experience all your feelings, accept your imperfections, and give yourself permission to grow—it means you recognize the polarities within yourself. You acknowledge to yourself and others that you have both strengths and weaknesses.

It also means you have set up a program to progressively move toward the quite reasonable and attainable objective, *not* of being perfect, but of being *whole!*

DO IT GOD'S WAY

In the process there will be highs and lows. Successes and failures. Hits and misses. Good times and bad. The question is: How do you deal with the lows? The failures? The misses? The bad times?

You can do it one of two ways. God's way—which Jesus makes clear in the second Beatitude is confession, repentance, and forgiveness—or Satan's way—which is self-condemnation and self-rejection leading to Satan's second anti-attitude: feelings of worthlessness.

WORTHLESSNESS AS CHRONIC REGRET

Jesus—who knows you're human and will blow it sometimes—accepts this quite human frailty in you. He invites you to employ God's provision for all such failures and be comforted. Satan says: "Oh, no! It isn't enough for you to be sorry for your sin. It isn't enough for you to mourn. You must punish yourself for being truly human. You must make sure you've done full penance for your humanness by continuing to feel bad about yourself."

If you believe the devil's lie, you slip into chronic regret. On the surface this may appear to be humility and repentance. Actually, it's inverted pride and unrepentance. A part of you looks down on the rest of you and condemns what it sees. You wind up feeling worthless and unfit for a place on this planet. You fall into the trap of universalizing your faults, globalizing your guilt, and feeling condemned on all counts at all times.

Cecil Osborne tells of a friend who had been struggling to overcome this sense of cosmic worthlessness. On one occasion this poor beleaguered fellow blurted out, "Why, if I were suddenly accused of starting World War II, I'd look up startled and say, 'Yes, but I didn't mean to!' "[1]

Satan is such a clever liar he can often make even the most ridiculous charges and impressions stick.

A little boy who had just moved to a new home with his family was out playing in the back yard. Suddenly he saw what he thought was a lion. Running into the house he yelled, "Mommy, Mommy, there's a lion in our yard."

"Oh, Sonny, that can't be."

"But, there is," he insisted, "I saw it. He's huge. And I heard him roar!"

The mother went out to the back yard with her boy

and said, "Son, that's not a lion. That's the neighbor's old shaggy dog."

The youngster wasn't fully convinced. So she said, "Tonight when you go to bed, you tell the Lord how frightened you were. Tell him how you thought that old shaggy dog was a lion. And ask him to help you see things as they are. That way you won't be frightened anymore."

Later that night the lad went to bed and dutifully said his prayers. In the morning his mother asked him if he'd followed her advice and talked to God about his fear. "Yes, Mom, I did. But do you know something? God told me that old shaggy dog almost had him fooled!"

Wouldn't it be great if we could always see things as they are? But Satan is such an outlandish liar that he's often able to trick reasonably healthy, halfway mature Christians into believing they are worthless. Hopeless. Better off dead. It's happened to me. Maybe it's happened to you.

REPENTANCE AND GODLY REGRET

The irony of it—the reason Satan can make it work—is that there is a place for godly regret in a healthy Christian's life. There are times when you need to mourn your sin—to be depressed by it to the point of repentance! But once an inner reconstruction has begun to take place through repentance and renewal, once you have felt enough pain to want to change, then godly sorrow has accomplished its purpose. To persist in that sorrow until it hardens into chronic regret is neither right nor good.

Once you have employed God's provision (confession, repentance, and forgiveness) for failure of all kinds, there is no further need for regret. You must not tolerate it five minutes longer. If you do, Satan will use it to generate a gnawing sense of uneasiness that God has not fully forgiven you and that he cannot unless you pay some staggering emotional price in the form of continuing unhappiness with yourself.

A man was walking home from work one winter day and decided to cut through the cemetery to save some time. In a moment of carelessness he fell into an open grave. The ground was frozen. He couldn't climb out and began yelling, "Get me out of here. I'm cold. Get me out of here. I'm cold."

The town inebriate was passing the cemetery and heard the yelling. He meandered over to see what the commotion was all about and found this fellow clawing at the side of the grave yelling, "Get me out of here. I'm cold. Get me out here. I'm cold." After surveying the situation for a moment, he responded, "Of course you're cold. You shook off all your dirt!"

Well, praise the Lord, our deliverance from the cold chill of exposure to the uglier aspects of our fallen nature is not dependent upon our shaking off any of the effects of a sinful past. In fact, it isn't dependent upon our doing anything for God. It only requires our joyful acceptance of what God has already done for us in Jesus.

WHAT IT REALLY MEANS TO BE SORRY

The prodigal son in our Lord's famous story honored his father, not by repining, but by rejoicing. Had he less faith in his father, he might have sat dejected in a corner—feeling worthless—instead of joining in the fun and festivity. Fortunately, his confidence in the loving-kindness of his father gave him the courage to reject those feelings of worthlessness. He was able to accept the fact he was acceptable to his father. For the first time in his checkered life he was happy—honest-to-goodness, deep-down happy.

And that's what God wants for you. He wants you to know what it really means to be sorry. Or, to put it in technical terms, he wants you to discern the difference between a shame-oriented conscience and a guilt-oriented conscience.

GUILT AND SHAME ARE NOT THE SAME

A shame-oriented conscience is one of the sad by-products of perfectionism. It is the residual effect of correction by parents, teachers, siblings, and other authority figures which focuses on the person rather than the deed. *"You're* bad," *"you're* stupid," instead of *"that's* bad," *"that's* stupid." As a consequence, one grows up feeling shame without any assurance that it's possible to be forgiven.

A guilt-oriented conscience recognizes that being truly human there will be times when you do things which are bad or stupid. But it knows forgiveness is available.

If you're saddled with a shame-oriented conscience, you can only go on feeling depressed. But if you possess a guilt-oriented conscience, you can say: "Guilty, but forgiven—praise the Lord!" As a result you begin to experience *makarios*. Happiness. The enviable state of joy in the Lord.

There is no *makarios* (the word translated "blessed") just because you cry. Feeling like a failure doesn't produce happiness. But if failure puts you on your knees where through confession and repentance you receive God's forgiveness, then forgiveness takes away the tears. *Makarios*—happiness—comes!

That's what I had in mind in writing the following paraphrase of Matthew 5:4:

Rx *for worthlessness: Happy are those who know what it really means to be sorry for their sin—who acknowledge the futility of chronic regret and actively employ God's provision (confession, repentance, and forgiveness) for failure of all kinds. They will be given the double cure of comfort and courage.*

TRUE CONFESSION

There's an ancient axiom which says: confession is good for the soul. That's true, if it's honest confession. And honest confession is not hyper-sensitivity to imaginary wrongs.

It's possible, you see, to become so sensitive—often because of the perfectionist tendencies in people around you—you're bullied into feeling guilty for no reason at all. But this is not honest confession. It's a kind of pious doormat-ism designed to make you look and feel more penitent than you really are. It's a kind of con job in which one deceives himself. Through false humility he succeeds in avoiding any real confrontation with the implications of what it means to be truly human.

Honest confession is simply taking God's side against your sin. It is calling it by its proper name: sin! It is saying, "God, I don't want this to be part of my life any more." If you can't say that—and let's admit that sometimes sin is fun, so the moment you're confessing it you're thinking about the next time you're going to do it—at least you can say, "God, I don't *want to* want this to be part of my life any more." That's honest. And honest confession, while not a healing, is a precondition for healing.

"If we confess our sins, He is faithful and righteous to forgive us our sins and to cleanse us from all unrighteousness" (1 John 1:9, NASB). I love that word "cleanse." It's like the good feeling of a hot shower after you've gotten grimy and sweaty from a day of hard work. Or the blessed feeling of released pressure when a boil is lanced, the infectious matter removed, and the wound sterilized so healing can begin.

"Confession is not the healing itself, rather it is the cleansing that allows the healing forces to begin their work."[2] When confession is followed by repentance, forgiveness comes with the dual cure of comfort and courage.

RUN, DON'T WALK!

Repentance is an action word. True sorrow for sin not only regrets the wrong behavior, it repents of it. It turns away from it. Therefore, if you know what it really means to mourn your sin, you will do a complete about-face. You will give up the tantalizing notion sin is something you can wink at. Play with. Fondle and have fun with. You will recognize sin is something you must flee from. And that means: run, don't walk!

When you do that, the "u" goes out of "mourning" leaving "morning." A new day. A new beginning. Bright. Clean. Inviting. Indeed: Happy are those who know what it really means to be sorry for sin—who acknowledge the futility of chronic regret and actively employ God's provision (confession, repentance and forgiveness) for failure of all kinds. They will be given the double cure of comfort and courage.

GOD'S DOUBLE CURE

The word translated "comforted" carries the added meaning of reassurance. I see Jesus promising true mourners comfort for the past, plus courage for the present and future.

God never meant sorrow for sin to put you down. He meant it to pick you up—to point you toward the incredible discovery God is for you, not against you. He wants you to enjoy both comfort and courage. Comfort in knowing that through confession and repentance the past is forgiven and forgotten. Courage to believe that through the energizing power of his Holy Spirit at work in you change can come in the now, and can continue to come in the future. Not because you think so. Hope so. Or guess so. But because God said so. "Blessed are those who mourn, for they *shall* be comforted" (Matt. 5:4,

NASB, italics mine). That's a promise from God. You can count on it.

BREAK DOWN THE BARRIERS

Someone has said, "Impression without expression leads to depression." Perhaps, as you've been reading, the Lord has impressed you with the possibility of a double cure, that is, comfort and courage. Now you must actualize it. You must make it your own.

Listed below are twenty-four wrong attitudes which can cause depression and constitute barriers to experiencing joy in the Lord:

anger (aggression)
anxiety
critical spirit
egocentricity
envy (discontentment)
fear
guilt
inferiority (worthlessness)
jealousy
lack of discipline
lack of love for God
lack of love for man
lack of trust
materialism (acquisitiveness)
physical laziness
pride (perfectionism)
procrastination
resentment
self-pity
sensitive spirit
sensuality (hedonism)
spiritual laziness

unforgiving nature (defensiveness)
unsurrendered will

Try to identify any of the above as being active in you. Select any you are ready to relinquish *now*. Tell God: "Father, I don't want to want _____ _____ to be part of my life any more." Thank him for hearing your honest confession and responding to this act of repentance. Guilty, but forgiven—praise the Lord!

THREE CHEERS FOR FORGIVENESS

One of the great books of all time, *Pilgrim's Progress*, has a beautiful passage expressing the incredible joy Christian, the main character in the story, feels when the burden of his sin finally rolls away. John Bunyan describes Christian climbing to the summit of Calvary. There, before the cross, he releases his sin into the loving, healing forgiveness of Almighty God. The burden rolls off his shoulders, tumbles down the hill, disappears into the open tomb and is lost forever. Then John Bunyan says, "Christian gave three leaps for joy, and went on singing."

Think of it. The man actually leaped for joy because he got saved. Can you imagine such "fanaticism"? I've seen people jump up and down because they won $5,000 or a new car on a TV game show. I've watched people "go bananas" at a football game because a player on their team caught a fifty-yard pass for a touchdown. But leap for joy because of forgiveness? Imagine it.

Yes! Please *do* imagine it. In fact, you may want to go so far as to actually *do* it. Now. Where you are. Or, if that's not possible, the moment you're in a place where it is possible.

Salvation is something to leap about. To shout about. To get excited about. If there's an element missing in much of evangelical Christianity today, it's excitement over what it means to be born again.

Gert Behenna says two things impressed her upon becoming a Christian: the incredible joy of being forgiven and the almost universal absence of joy in the average Christian. As I reflected on her comment I decided to see if I could do something about it in the church I pastor.

I'm a frustrated high school yell leader. So one Sunday morning I concluded my sermon by suggesting we give three cheers for forgiveness. And did we ever! Followed by whistles, shouts of joy, and thunderous applause we yelled:

Guilty, but forgiven—praise the Lord!
Guilty, but forgiven—praise the Lord!
Guilty, but forgiven—praise the Lord!

If anyone had told me I'd do a thing like that in a stately, dignified, mainline, Sunday morning church service, I would have suggested they were "going 'round the bend." But it proved to be one of the most therapeutic things we have ever done. All week long folks went out of their way to express how much it had meant to them. "For the first time in my life I *feel* forgiven," many said.

In the case of some, real healing took place. They released inner tensions and "let the child out" in a healthy way by creating a condition which permitted the message of God's acceptance to "get through." Their ears heard their mouth say: "Guilty, but forgiven—praise the Lord!" At long last they really *believed* it! If they could share personally with you, they'd say: "Try it. It works!"

5

GET OFF THE FENCE

Happy are those who claim nothing, for the whole earth will belong to them! Matthew 5:5

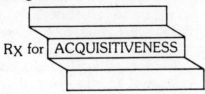

Rx for ACQUISITIVENESS

When you mount a ladder, you place your foot first on one rung and then the next. At your discretion you move up or down, rung by rung, till you reach the desired level. Then you get busy doing whatever it was that caused you to get on the ladder in the first place.

The Beatitudes are like that. Arranged in a series of rungs—each leading to the next—they will, if you apply them, lift you level by level toward the goal of happiness here and now.

Similarly the anti-attitudes Satan offers are also like a ladder. They, too, are arranged in sequence. They, too, progress like a series of rungs. In this case, however, instead of leading upward into joy, they lead you downward into depression.

The first of these anti-attitudes is perfectionism. The illusion you *can* and therefore *should* be supernormal. More than OK. Virtually flawless.

Failure to reach this unachievable objective triggers a flood-tide of bad feelings about yourself, summed up best in Satan's second anti-attitude: worthlessness.

Then, promising to assuage these feelings of worthlessness, Satan takes advantage of your increasing vulnerability to misdirection and presents you with his third anti-attitude: acquisitiveness.

Before you know it, you are frantically engaged in a feverish effort to acquire all the obvious evidences of worth, all the things the world says will make you a person of significance—money, fame, power, position, possessions.

But instead of producing the desired effect, acquisitiveness only makes you anxious and frustrated. It isn't long before you realize you are investing your whole search for meaning in things which are transient in their appeal. Temporary in their ability to satisfy. And, most frightening of all, terribly susceptible to loss.

Even though you are less and less fulfilled, and more and more aware of the futility of acquisitiveness, the mere thought of losing it all is terrifying. So you hurl yourself with even greater intensity into a struggle to keep what you've got and, if possible, get more.

The consequence: overstress with the inevitable depletion of any physical or emotional reserve you may have, resulting in depression.

Someone has said the modern American is one who drives a bank-financed car over a bond-financed highway on credit card gas to open a charge account at a department store so he can fill his savings and loan-financed home with installment-purchased furniture!

All of this cannot be done with immunity. There's a payday some day, as attested to by the sign hanging outside a bankruptcy court: "Attention, please. You finally caught up with the Joneses."

ACQUISITIVENESS AND LEVELS OF STRESS

A certain amount of stress is desirable, in fact necessary, for healthy achievement. Underload can be as regrettable as overload. Controlled stress makes possible most of our progress. But overstress should be recognized for the danger it is. In chapter three I mentioned hearing a lecture on stress by Dr. M. Roberts Grover, dean of instruction at the University of Oregon Medical School. He used a graphic called "Your Stress Tank."[1] Below is an adaptation devised by Janet Shaw, a gifted commercial artist who works on our staff. We've called it "Your Stressmobile." The wheels indicate stress is part of the "machinery" of your life which allows you to progress toward worthy and attainable goals.

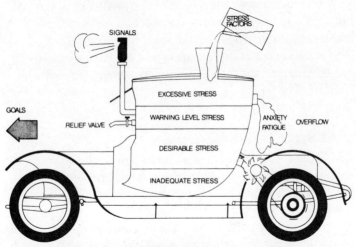

"Your Stressmobile" adapted by Janet Shaw

At the top is an opening through which "stress factors" are poured. At the bottom is a level identified as "inadequate stress." At this level you are without pressure. You also aren't going anywhere! There isn't enough of the energy created by stress to push you forward.

The second level labeled "desirable stress" is, as we shall see, the equivalent of "meekness" (Matt. 5:5), which really means "power under control." The spigot on the right allows the energy created by "desirable stress" to be

released in a controlled, directed way. This activates the
drive shaft and moves your "stressmobile" toward worthy
and attainable goals.

The next stage called "warning level stress" is where
you have reached a state of overstress. Certain signals
begin to appear. Such things as feelings and bodily
reactions which are new and troubling. Or nondisabling
symptoms like forgetfulness and indecisiveness.

A man went to his doctor. "Do you have trouble
making decisions?" the physician asked. To which the
man replied, "Well, yes and no."

The signals are warnings that overstress is present. But
notice the valve on the left. It's there to suggest there
are creative ways to relieve stress. Healthy satisfactions.
Positive diversions. "Alternative sources of self-esteem,"
as Dr. Grover calls them. What Jesus identified as being
"meek" (Matt. 5:5).

WAYS TO LOWER STRESS

Dr. Grover and his associates have developed a list of
sixty-six safety valves—little satisfactions and diversions
you can give yourself to lower stress.[2] Here are a few:
a walk in the twilight or early morning. Sharing a fun
experience with a friend or a child. Gardening—especially
pulling weeds. (That doesn't appeal to me at all!)
Travel—doing it or thinking about it. A long, hot bubble
bath. Visiting a friend or neighbor you seldom see. Doing
absolutely nothing. (Now that appeals to me!) Deep
breathing for relaxation. Listening to music. Going
barefoot. Reading. Going hunting. Jogging. Baking bread.
Going out to a new restaurant. Watching a sunset.
Singing with a group. Flying a kite. Taking a nap.
(Another of my favorites!)

All of these are creative diversions or satisfactions (little
rewards, if you want to call them that) for having borne
enough of life's burdens to raise the stress to the "warning

level." By employing one or more of these creative "relief valves" you can lower stress to a desirable level. If you don't both input and buildup continue until you reach a state of "excessive stress," or what Dr. Grover calls "disabling overflow." This is expressed in anxiety and/or fatigue which provide little or no driving force. They just spill out. Should any of this "disabling overflow" hit the drive shaft of your "stressmobile" not much happens. The energy is gone. You are virtually immobilized.

ACQUISITIVENESS, OVERSTRESS, AND DEPRESSION

So pervasive is acquisitiveness—Satan's third anti-attitude—that the resulting overstress is well nigh universal. So is the neurotic depression it causes. If you're being bugged by it, please understand it comes from putting your trust in things which are ultimately untrustworthy. Things that cannot see you through. And by "through" I mean all the way through—to the end—and beyond.

The net effect of overstress is eventual depression, as I learned to my own chagrin some years ago. The 1960s were difficult for all of us. I was no exception. There was a high degree of anti-institutionalism and social unrest. Nationally we faced tons of anxiety. Individually I was drowning. Or so it seemed.

My wife had broken her leg in a skiing accident and was in a cast for eleven months, placing a great deal of stress on both of us.[3] There was a suicide in our immediate family. I ran into personal and vocational problems I never thought could happen to me. For the first time in twenty-five years of ministry, the crowds were not larger than the year before. The offerings fell off slightly. Evidences of inner agitation began to appear. I was less understanding with my wife and children. I began to experience a decline in physical prowess. Fatigue accompanied by sleeplessness developed. I would fall into bed exhausted, sleep for about an hour or two, wake up startled and lie there the rest of the night staring into the darkness contemplating what a failure I was.

I recognized the seriousness of all this, talked to a physician friend, and asked him to recommend somebody I could see. He mentioned the name of an endocrinologist in Los Angeles whom I immediately consulted, spelling out my symptoms. After a bunch of tests and a couple of weeks of evaluation, I saw him a second time.

"There's no question but what your body chemistry is out of 'sync.' Your adrenal hormone level is exceptionally high. Usually," he went on, "when people have this combination of physical factors, they complain of depression."

"Didn't I mention that to you?"

"No, you didn't."

"Oh, yes," I said. "I slip into depression every Sunday evening and remain that way most of Monday. I figured it was part of the price of being a preacher, sort of postpartum blues, as I give birth to a sermon each week."

He nodded knowingly as I likened it to gals who go through all the effort, pain, and struggle of producing a baby, present it to people who look, smile, say, "Isn't that nice," and go on about their business.

Many preachers go through that every week because, while preaching looks easy, it isn't. It's not easy to stand in the same place and talk to the same people on the same subject year after year, hopefully making it interesting, challenging, and inspiring. However, you do the best you can. You present your "baby," and people say, "Gee, that's nice." Then they go home, have dinner, maybe a second piece of pie, belch, take a nap, and when they wake up they've forgotten everything you said. After a few years of that you begin to wonder: "What am I? A kind of glorified *hausfrau* fixing food for hungry people?"

Frankly, that's how I came to terms with my case of

recurring postpartum blues. I decided I am a spiritual
hausfrau with not only the job—*but the privilege*—of
preparing food for spiritually hungry people. And I try to
make it as tasty as possible.

So I said, "Doctor, I understand the Sunday night and
Monday deal. What I don't understand is why I feel so
depressed the first five to seven days of my vacation."
At one time we owned a lake lodge in the northwoods of
Wisconsin. I loved it there. The water, trees, and clear
blue sky combined to create a virtual paradise. And yet
the first week of vacation was torturous for me.

I told him about one time in particular. It was a
gorgeous day. Blue sky. Green trees. Clean, crisp air.
The lake glistened in the sun as a gentle breeze played
across the surface of the water. It was beautiful. Yet there
I was driving down the country road which passed our
place, tears rolling down my cheeks, saying, "What's
wrong with me? Why can't I enjoy this?"

I drove the fifteen miles into town where I met Harry
Pride, a delightful red-faced Irish friend of mine.
"How are you doing?" he asked.

"To be honest, Harry, I feel terrible."

"I feel that way sometimes," he went on. "I get so
depressed I crawl under the bed. Ginny (that's his wife)
gets down, pokes around with a broomstick and says,
'Come on out, Harry, it'll be all right.' And it is,"
he added.

We got into his car, mosied down the road about eight
miles an hour, made a couple of turns, and wound up in
the cemetery. "Why'd you bring me here?" I asked.

"Oh, I just thought you'd like to see a whole pile of
people who used to have problems like yours. They don't
anymore. Do you want to trade places with them?" I got
the message.

The doctor explained the reason for this period of
depression after months of intense pressure. "You have
been through so many crises vocationally and personally—

plus your weekly sermonic birthing process—your adrenal
glands keep pumping in hormone to help you through the
crises and then all of a sudden you stop. Your adrenal
glands haven't gotten the message that these crises are
over and so, as sometimes happens to the throttle of a
car, they get stuck open. They continue to pump
hormone into your system, producing endogenous
depression. Finally they get the message, stop, and
everything's cool. You feel fine again."

Having dealt with my "vacation syndrome," we talked
further about my other, more persistent symptoms. They
were physical all right, but I began to see them as related
to neurotic depression. As a perfectionist I wanted to
please everyone—all the time. Failing to do so I tried
harder. The harder I tried the less successful I was.

I remember one fellow who was concerned about our
Sunday evening service. This was several years ago.

Our staff planned what we thought were super-terrific
services. We had fantastic themes. Glorious music. A little
group activity mixed in to make everybody participants,
not just spectators. But because it didn't fit this man's
concept of what a Sunday evening service should be, he
kept his family home for twenty-seven Sunday nights in
a row!

Every Monday I would awaken at 2 A.M. wondering:
"What do I have to do to please this fellow?" I would get
angry at him. Then my anger would retroflex back on me
and I'd get all kinds of bad feelings about myself. What a
failure I was and the like. I remember saying to Lucille,
"Honey, there just isn't a market for a minister who wants
to hew to the broad middle. People want you to be over
on this extreme or that. They don't want somebody who's
sensitive to the extremes, but stays in the middle where I
believe the gospel is. There just isn't a market for me!"
And I came close to quitting the ministry at that time.

Then I said, "No! I'll try harder. I'll work harder. I'll
acquire all the evidences of a successful minister. We'll go

after bigger crowds and sufficient funds to expand the ministry." So I started into that whirlwind again. I became more and more frayed. Anxious. Depressed. Physically depleted.

Healing finally came when I decided I would no longer try to please everyone. I couldn't do it anyway. So why try! I told myself, "Don't set out to displease people. But, if in the process of doing what you feel is God's will for the church, you do displease people—so be it." In other words, I found at least part of my answer in Matthew 5:5: "Blessed are the meek, for they shall inherit the earth." Later I paraphrased it in the form of a prescription:

RX *for acquisitiveness: Happy are those who claim nothing—who recognize overstress when they see it, abandon the world's way of determining one's worth, and live with eternity's values in view. The whole earth will belong to them.*

SUCCESS FORMULA PAR EXCELLENCE

This is the most astonishing success formula ever devised. And it's particularly astonishing to us Americans because we have such a warped idea of what meekness is. As I said above, meekness is that desirable level of stress wherein you have "power under control." It's that very special kind of effectiveness which really makes the world go 'round in the best sense of the phrase.

The Greeks used the word *praos*—translated "meek" in Matthew 5:5—to describe wild horses which had been tamed and were therefore useful to their master. Thus, in the truest sense, the meek are God-tamed people. Just as a wild horse is caught, haltered, bridled, and gentled until it becomes useful to its master, so, too, our wild nature must be tamed by God before we are of practical and constructive use to him.

As someone has pointed out, "the bull in the china

shop smashing the beautiful objects of art has strength—the strength of a bull. The bully in the crowd elbowing his way to the front and bowling over his weaker brethren has strength—the strength of a bully."[4] But the strength of which Jesus speaks in this third Beatitude is like the power produced when the Niagara River is harnassed and its wild, rushing flow is used to produce electricity.

Or, as someone else has suggested, it's like the jujitsu expert who knows his own strength and therefore doesn't have to go around proving anything to anyone. When he's threatened, he stands quietly—watchfully waiting for a bull-like charge. Then, instead of destroying his adversary, he catches and grips him in such a way that he cannot storm or rage any longer, and in that moment the adversary discovers he has met his master.[5]

Even so, the meek are those who know their own strength (which is really God's strength flowing in and through them) and thus are masters of life situations. Indeed, happy are those who claim nothing. They have lost the need to be anything other than who they are—imperfect people with room to grow. Guilty, but forgiven—praise the Lord! Thus they are able to relax and be at ease with themselves.

They have learned, or are learning, what Paul says in Philippians 4:11, 12: ". . . I have *learned* to be content in whatever circumstances I am. I know how to get along with humble means, and I also know how to live in prosperity; in any and every circumstance I have *learned* the secret of being filled and going hungry, both of having abundance and suffering need" (NASB, italics mine).

AN ALTERNATIVE TO ACQUISITIVENESS

Actually there are two ways to gain and maintain self-esteem. The first is through power and achievement—

acquisitiveness. The second is through love and relationship—meekness. Satan and society train and set you up for the first with its ugly consequences. God wants to release you from that pressure by teaching you to be meek. He wants to help you achieve a level of self-love and self-acceptance, which allows you to be content with who you are and what you have.

LEARN TO IDENTIFY SYMPTOMS OF OVERSTRESS

This will free you, as our prescription says, to recognize the symptoms of overstress when you see them. Ailments of one sort or another. Mild recurring depression. An absence of joy. I can look back now and see how my personal spiritual goal of several years ago—to find fifty-two evidences of God's sense of humor—was a signal that my stress level was getting too high. I was trying to find a creative relief valve to let off some of the pressure.

Another evidence of overstress is the inability to find time to relax. If you're too busy to play, you're too busy! Harold Walker talks about the principle of alternation which seems to be a law of life. He says, "There is a need for both driving ahead and pausing to find the way, for movement and for meditation. The archer hits his target both by pulling and by letting go. He brings the bow to stern tension and then lets it relax."[6] He hits the target through the principle of alternation.

A little lady from the hill country was celebrating her one-hundredth birthday. Someone asked her secret. Our uptight age could learn much from her reply: "When I works, I works hard. When I sets, I sets loose." An inability to "set loose" is an evidence of overstress which needs to be dealt with.

Another indication is an increasing use of and dependence upon non-creative diversions such as sick sex, alcohol, prescription drugs. In the case of endogenous depression—which is internal and physical—the psychic energizers available today are remarkably effective. Medically monitored, they are wonderfully helpful and good.

But no amount of alcohol, phenobarbitol, or any other tranquilizer will succeed in helping you successfully combat overstress for long. It can only be done, as our prescription says, by abandoning the world's way of determining one's worth and living with eternity's values in view.

CHANGE THE REASON WHY YOU DO THINGS

When you abandon the world's way of determining worth, it doesn't mean you must change what you do so much as why you do it. You're not out there to prove anything anymore. What other people *think* isn't important, because you're in touch with what God *knows* about you. You no longer have a need to prop yourself up with pretentions.

"Blessed are the meek," Jesus said, "for they shall inherit the earth." Put that together with everything else he said about earthly possessions (a subject about which he said a great deal), and you realize he was not saying "don't acquire," he was saying "acquire things in the right way for the right reason." In other words, learn to live with eternity's values in view.

"The reason you can't find any satisfaction through the acquiring of earth's treasure is not because the world is too big for you, but because you're too big for the world."[7] There isn't one thing in this world which will last. But in Christ *you* will. That's why it makes all kinds of sense to exchange what you cannot keep for what you cannot lose. "For what does it profit a man to gain the whole world, and forfeit his soul?" (Mark 8:36). The world isn't worth losing your soul for, because the world won't last.

GET A NEW PERSPECTIVE ON LIFE

Live and give with eternity's values in view. This may require developing a new perspective toward life. The puzzle printed below suggests how. Take a pencil and, without lifting it from the paper, see if you can connect all nine dots with only four straight lines.

If you have trouble working the puzzle, the answer is printed on page 71. What's involved, you see, is the principle of extending your perception. Of looking beyond the obvious. Spiritually, it's learning to live and to give with eternity's values in view.

On my office wall, by the door where I see it every time I leave, is a motto which reads: "The only way to overcome the tyranny of money is to ruthlessly give it away." I don't have a lot of money. I have more than I ever thought I would when I entered the ministry. For that I praise the Lord and thank friends who have given me wise counsel. But one doesn't have to have a lot of money to be tyrannized by it. And, I've learned the only way to overcome its tyranny is to ruthlessly give it away. It's living and giving with eternity's values in view which helps to keep things in proper perspective. For those who so live and give, Jesus said, "The whole earth will belong to them" (Phillips translation).

The word Jesus used here is beautiful. It refers to this good earth. The original Greek word doesn't mean the cosmos. It doesn't mean the universe. It doesn't mean the kingdom of God. It means solid dirt. This earth!

What Jesus is saying is that if you become one who claims nothing, you'll get the whole earth as a gift. Having given it over to God, he will give it back to you with new freedom to enjoy it. To have it or not have it. But either way, as Paul said, "To be content" (Phil. 4:11). You will be a happy user of all God richly gives (1 Tim. 6:17). You will be able to possess without being possessed. To own without being owned. And by acknowledging his ownership over everything, there is a sense in which you will become invulnerable to the loss of those things which don't matter anyway.

Truly, this is the most incredible success formula ever fashioned. If it had come from a lesser person, you might chuck it. You might laugh it out of court. You might dismiss it as stupid and fanciful. But coming as it does from Jesus, who put together the most successful life ever lived, you have to take it seriously: Give it all up and you'll get it back with new freedom to enjoy it.

HOW ONE MAN CONQUERED ACQUISITIVENESS

Jim Newton is a fascinating fellow. I met him on a Bibleland Cruise. During a lull in our sightseeing schedule, he shared his walk with the Lord. He described how, as a young bachelor, working in New England as a salesman, he was self-motivated, self-driven, self-directed, and determined to be a self-made success. One night, after working all day without a sale, he returned to his hotel room. He looked in the mirror and said, "Are you a man or a mouse?" He decided he was a man and made up his mind then and there to never again leave a town without selling somebody something—regardless of what it took! And that's what he did.

One evening he was in Augusta, Maine. A dance was

scheduled in the hotel where he was staying. He was single. He liked to dance. So he went to the room where he supposed the dance was being held and found a group of people sitting in a circle. He thought they were getting acquainted. He went in, sat down, and listened as they told a bit about themselves. When it came his turn he introduced himself. Told what he did. Where he was from. That sort of thing.

Then a young man stood and began to tell how his life had been changed through a personal relationship with Jesus Christ. Jim Newton told me he sat there and listened to that young man. The more he heard the more he realized that what this chap was talking about was what Jim had been searching for all his life.

After the meeting he approached the speaker and said, "If I accept Jesus as my Savior and Lord tonight, what will I have to do tomorrow?" The man said, "I don't know. But if you accept Jesus tonight, tomorrow you'll know!"

Jim Newton made a serious commitment to Jesus that night. He named him both Savior and Lord. In the morning he entered the hotel dining room with an envelope. On it he had scribbled a couple thoughts. He handed the envelope to his newfound friend and said, "What do you think? Does that look like guidance to you?"

The man looked at it, handed it back and said, "What do you think?" Jim Newton said, "I think God wants me to go to my former boss and return some money I swiped from him, money I thought I deserved, but really didn't. Second, I think God wants me to go to my customers and tell them I've been less than truthful with them."

"I did the first," Jim said simply, "and started on the second. Near the top of my list was my biggest customer. I asked for an appointment, told him what had happened to me and that I had been less than truthful with him. He looked at me and said, 'Mr. Newton, weren't you afraid to tell me this? Weren't you afraid you were going to lose my business?' Yes, sir, I was afraid, but not that I would lose your business. I was afraid you would lose respect for me. 'Well, Mr. Newton,' the man replied, 'you've been honest with me. Let me be honest with you. Until a few moments ago when you told me what you did, I didn't have any respect for you!'"

Jim Newton went on to become very successful as a salesman. He was able to dedicate roughly twenty years of his life as a missionary without salary. When time came to retire he was out of money. He decided to move to Florida and use a real estate license he had acquired. His goal was to make just enough for himself and Ellie, his wife, to live out their lives in comfort.

"I'm going to make this a Christian business, Ellie. We're going to run it on Christian principles. I believe God will bless us."

"And he did," Jim added quietly. Soon he had a number of salesmen. Business was booming. "Then, John, something hit me. I realized three of my best salesmen—their combined sales amounted to several million dollars annually—were not being completely truthful. They were chipping the corners off the cube of truth so it would roll in their favor.

"I hate to tell you how I struggled with that," Jim said wistfully. "It should have been an easier decision. But, John, I walked around the block several times one day before I reaffirmed my decision to run a Christian business—whatever the cost. I went back to my office and, though I needed those salesmen and their production badly, I let them go." With a smile Jim concluded, "God honored that decision. Before we were through our sales that year were better than the year before. And they've been better every year since."

As I think of Jim Newton's story, I'm reminded of a famous line from the pen of C. S. Lewis: "Aim at heaven and you'll get earth thrown in. Aim at the earth and you'll get neither." Which means we've come to a most critical point in God's cure for depression. A decision is called for. A decision to stay on or get off the fence. You can't have it both ways. It's either acquisitiveness and the ultimate despair it brings, or it's meekness and release from pressure with freedom to enjoy. Which will it be?

In the diary of Longfellow there's an interesting statement. He returned home from church one Sunday and made the notation: "Our pastor preached a fine sermon." Then he added these destiny-determining words: "I applied it to myself." Will you do the same?

Answer to the puzzle printed on page 67.

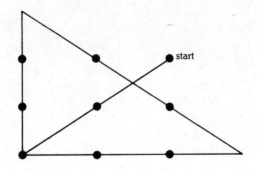

6

BREAK OUT OF BOREDOM

Happy are those who are hungry and thirsty for true goodness, for they will be fully satisfied! Matthew 5:6

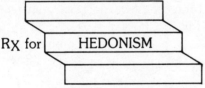

Rx for HEDONISM

Have you ever been gripped by the dynamic of a desperate desire? Something inside you demanding to be satisfied? If so, you know that whatever captures your attention captures you. Whatever succeeds in occupying your thoughts ultimately controls your life. As the ancient axiom expresses it:

Sow a thought, reap a deed,
Sow a deed, reap a habit.
Sow a habit, reap a character.
Sow a character, reap a life.

   Properly applied, this principle of the dynamic of a desperate desire can have a powerful and positive effect on mental health producing joy. Misapplied, it will have a powerful and negative effect resulting in depression. Let me show you how it works.

TRUE SATISFACTION OR HEDONISM?

Having led you ever so cleverly down the primrose path from perfectionism to worthlessness to acquisitiveness— each step resulting in more and more pain—at just the right moment (his timing is almost flawless!) the adversary suggests you need some relief from the strain under which you've been living. "You've been working hard to prove your worth! You deserve to be pampered," he says enticingly. With that thought he presents his fourth anti-attitude: hedonism—the quite beguiling notion that the aggressive pursuit of pleasure as an end in itself will lift your growing depression and relieve your pain.

Now the subtlety of that—the reason he can pull it off successfully—is that there's a legitimate place for pleasure in the life of a Spirit-filled Christian. Look again at "Your Stressmobile."

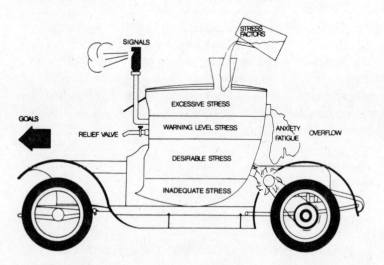

"Your Stressmobile" adapted by Janet Shaw

At the lowest level there is "inadequate stress" which is an undesirable state unless you're on vacation! There isn't any pressure at this level, but neither is there any progress. There isn't enough of the energy created by stress to move the "machinery" of your life toward worthy goals.

At the second level, however, is "desirable stress." This is, as I explained in chapter five, the equivalent of meekness—"power under control." Directed toward the drive shaft it moves your "stressmobile" toward desirable goals.

Then there is "warning level stress." At this point you are in a state of overstress. Signals are going off in the form of feelings and physical reactions which are less than good. There is a valve there, too, labeled "relief valve." It suggests there are several ways to creatively lower stress to the desirable, functioning, energizing level.

GOD'S SYSTEM
FOR ACHIEVING SELF-ESTEEM

Perhaps the best way is to develop an alternate system of achieving self-esteem. Satan's method is acquisitiveness. It places ever-increasing pressure upon you to get more and more of the things you need less and less. The result is depression. *The purpose of this book—the bottom line at which I am aiming—is to introduce you to an alternate system of achieving self-esteem. This is what we have in "the blessed attitudes" of Jesus (Matt. 5:3-10).*

That takes time. It may require building a new life style. The immediacy of overstress may discourage you. With warning signals going off, you may feel something has to give—now! Well, there are a couple of things you can do—right now—to relieve the immediate situation and give yourself time to take long-term corrective action.

You can employ a position distraction. Take a walk. Go for a drive. Read a book. Watch a ball game on TV.

Or, you can indulge in a wholesome satisfaction—some little pleasure—which will have the net effect of lowering your level of stress.

One Saturday I awakened very early. A dozen things were clamoring for my attention, so I got up, made some hospital calls and headed for the office. A pile of correspondence had accumulated due to my travel schedule. After four hours of nonstop dictation I reached the bottom of the pile. The needs, desires, and requests which had come to me were voluminous. But I was done. It felt good!

Then it hit me. Sunday's sermon still had to be prepared. I had done the initial thinking (and some of the research) on the plane earlier in the week. But, as every preacher knows, there's a good deal more to sermon preparation than just thinking about it! The stress level began to get high. I knew I couldn't work well in that state. So I practiced what I preached. I took a nap! When I awakened a half hour later, I was refreshed and ready to give God my best.

Wholesome satisfactions—simple little pleasures—are healthy and good. They are in keeping with your higher nature. Having been made in the image of God you are—in the highest sense of the term—made for pleasure!

YOUR GOD-GIVEN CAPACITY FOR PLEASURE

I have already shown you God is a happy God. In 1 Timothy 1:11 Paul used the same word in reference to God which Jesus used in the Beatitudes: "blessed." It means happy. So your God is a happy, joyful God.

But did you realize he also has a capacity for pleasure? Numerous passages throughout the Bible refer to this interesting attribute of God. The Psalms speak of him as taking pleasure in his people. Philippians 2:13 says he is at work in us "for his good pleasure." The *King James*

Version speaks of the whole creation having been brought into being "for his pleasure" (Rev. 4:11).

Yours is a happy God with a capacity for pleasure. You were made in his image (Gen. 1:26). So you, too, have a natural, God-given capacity for pleasure. Pleasure fulfills one of the needs with which you were born.

Satan, who is aware of our need, distorts this quite normal desire. By exaggerating its importance he promotes the anti-attitude of hedonism—the idea that pleasure is the sole or chief goal in life.

But this, too, is self-defeating. Hedonism in its uglier forms is a dead-end street. As Dr. Bernard Idding Bell points out: "Man is an animal which alone among the animals refuses to be satisfied by the fulfillment of animal desires."[1]

The prodigal son in the far country of self-indulgence began at last to experience "rigor mortis of the spirit."[2] He was bored stiff with his pursuit of pleasure. Which is to say the most devastating discovery about hedonism in the form of pleasure run amuck—that in the end it is utterly, dreadfully, and depressingly boring!

And, as many of us have discovered, more of the same only leads to a greater sense of insufferable boredom. As one writer has said: "Many attempt to escape it by exciting their senses through drugs, alcohol, the misuse of sex. Many plunge into a self-gratifying orgy of buying bigger and better 'things.' But the roller coaster ends at the same terminal."[3]

HEDONISM LEAVES NO WAY OUT

Jean-Paul Sartre wrote a play called *No Exit*. It's about two women and a man in hell. Hell in Sartre's play turns out to be an ordinary, pleasant, comfortable room in which there is no door. No window. No means of escape. Forever these three people are locked up with each other—and their boredom—with no hope of getting out.

That's the hell of it in Sartre's play. And that's the hell of it on earth. Hedonism puts you in a room without windows. In a room without doors. In a state of boredom from which there is no relief.

Hedonism won't make it. You can drink and drink at the saltwater pleasures of this world and still die of thirst. You can gorge yourself on the husks of sin, masquerading as pleasure, and still die of hunger. If you adopt an increasingly jaded view of morality and ethics expressed in self-destructive acts, instead of being more and more satisfied you will become more and more unsatisfied. And along with it will come a deep sense of dread as you think the unthinkable thought: "My word! If none of this will satisfy, what on earth will?"

HOW TO BREAK OUT OF BOREDOM

There's hope! You can break out of boredom. God doesn't want you to live *for* pleasure, but he ever so much wants you to live *with* pleasure. He wants to set you free from neurotic depression rooted in perfectionism, worthlessness, acquisitiveness, and hedonism with its boring, unsatisfying concept of pleasure.

One way to do that is by faithfully following Christ's formula for joy: "Blessed are those who hunger and thirst for righteousness, for they shall be satisfied" (Matt. 5:6). Paraphrased as a prescription it works out as follows:

RX *for hedonism: Happy are those who are hungry and thirsty for righteousness — who, as a life style, deeply desire to please God, the only One worth pleasing. They will naturally, spontaneously, and enthusiastically become more and more whole.*

RIGHTEOUSNESS AS RIGHT-WISE-NESS

When I first wrote that prescription, I substituted "goodness" for "righteousness," because I felt the latter had grown flabby with age and had taken on an aura of arrogance which turns many people off. However, as I studied it further for this book, I came to see "righteousness" as a word with verve and virility. It has a keen, clean-cutting edge to it. It speaks of right-wise-ness. Of the quality or state of being right. Of being solid. Of being together. Of being whole.

When used in the Bible with reference to God, it speaks of God being himself. It describes God doing that which is consistent with God's nature. And the same is true with you. You were made in the image of God. For you to hunger and thirst after righteousness is for you to seek after that which eliminates the conflicts within you, because righteousness is consistent with your higher nature. In the deepest sense, righteousness fulfills the goal for which you were created. Thus it is something for which you should hunger and thirst.

"Hunger and thirst" are strong words. They are driving, intense words. Jesus wasn't talking about a loose, limp, casual, half-hearted, luke-warm notion or fancy. He wasn't describing a vague preference for "the good life." He wasn't referring to a happy-go-lucky "swinging-on-a-star" philosophy which hopes that someday you will somehow be somewhat better than you are. He was depicting the dynamic of a desperate desire. A yearning. A longing. A nagging in your soul which will not be denied.

RIGHTEOUSNESS AND JOY

This hungering and thirsting for righteousness is not a means of making yourself acceptable to God. Rather, it's an expression of joy at discovering you *are* acceptable to God. By being joyfully human (that is, able to succeed without undue pride and to fail without undue despair), you come to know what sorrow really means. To mourn in the healthy sense.

By surrendering any need to prove yourself to God

or anybody else, you reach a level in which your unquenchable desire—your hunger and thirst—is to please your loving Father who longs, *for your sake,* that you increasingly enjoy the state of being right. Of being together. Of being more and more whole.

Thus righteousness becomes the set of your sail. The direction in which you are pointed. There may be times when you drift off your heading, but these need not permanently alter your course. They are only momentary. "Habits wear off more easily than they drop off."[4] So keep at it. Set your sail. Tack this way or that if you must. But keep at it. The life style at which you are aiming is to please God, the only one worth pleasing—a purpose well worth pursuing.

IS YOUR GOD TOO SMALL?

The reason many people fail to find the joy of the Lord is that they do not go far enough to really know God as he is. In the book entitled *When God Says You're OK,* Jon Tal Murphree talks about some of the false concepts of God which are obstacles to a joyful and meaningful relationship with him.[5]

He describes the tyrant God who is "a cosmic combination of a prosecuting attorney, a prejudiced jury and an unrelenting judge all in one person"—a kind of "state trooper with a billy club in hand." At the other end of the spectrum he has "the good-old-boy God." A kind of jovial backslapper who delights in being taken advantage of. Then Jon Murphree quotes a little girl's letter to God in which she uses the words of a popular TV show: "Will the real Mr. God stand up?"

If your god is too small, you can discover God as he is by seeing him revealed in Jesus. Because whatever else God is he is nothing less than Jesus. When you see him revealed in Jesus, you know he is neither a tyrant nor a pushover. He is the personification of loving authority. A father who cares enough to exercise authority with love so you can enjoy life at its best.

You have only one judge: God! He never wags his finger at you. He only beckons you to come do it his way. Not for his sake—for your sake! He knows his way is the only way life will work out for you. As C. S. Lewis says in *Mere Christianity,* "God designed the human machine to run on himself. He himself is the fuel our spirits were designed to burn, or the food our spirits were designed to feed on. There isn't any other." Indeed: happy are those who are hungry and thirsty for righteousness. Who, as a life style, deeply desire to please God—the only One worth pleasing. They will naturally, spontaneously, and enthusiastically become more and more whole.

At the end of 2 Corinthians 5:21 we read this astounding statement: "We . . . become the righteousness of God in him [Jesus]." That is to say, in Jesus you naturally, spontaneously, and enthusiastically become more and more whole. In Jesus you are all God requires and desires you to be. In Jesus you are all you can never be on your own.

It happens naturally. Righteousness is imputed to you. The nature of Christ is put in you by God's grace and you begin to grow by the power of an inner-life principle which can only produce growth.

It happens spontaneously. Righteousness is imparted to you. And this gift of God's love makes possible a different life style just for the taking.

It happens enthusiastically. Righteousness is implanted in you. This new life principle is set deeply and securely in you, so righteousness becomes important to you. You want to spurn evil—not to get strokes from God, but to let him know how deeply you love and appreciate him. "I have to" is replaced by "I want to." When that happens you break out of boredom. You enter into joy. Naturally, spontaneously, and enthusiastically you become more and more whole.

Ruth Calkin, one of my favorite poets, says it so well:

Lord
There are countless things in my life
That are inexcusable.
There are things unaccountable
And things unexplainable.
There are things irrefutable
And things irresponsible.
But it comes to me with unutterable relief
That because of your love
Nothing in my life is unforgiveable![6]

7

BE REAL AND HEAL!

Happy are the merciful, for they will have mercy shown to them! Matthew 5:7

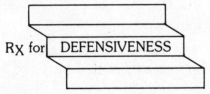

Rx for DEFENSIVENESS

Depression doesn't just happen. It always has a cause. It can be due to something internal and physical—a mixup in your body chemistry—and is called endogenous depression. Or, to something external and situational—a circumstance beyond your control, usually involving a sense of loss—and is called exogenous depression. Or, it's internal and attitudinal—a crossfire of conflicting emotions with you in the middle—and is called neurotic depression.

No one is immune to depression. Like the common cold, it strikes everyone at some time or other in one form or other. And you are quite unrealistic if you assume it can never happen to you. For sooner or later it will.

I'm thinking right now of a cartoon I saw some time ago. It showed a sinking boat. As the aft end settled, a group of concerned people gathered around a hole in the bottom through which water was rushing in. High and dry on the bow sat several complacent folk looking down at the others. The caption beneath the cartoon read: "My, aren't we fortunate the leak is not at our end!"

Well, we're all in the same boat when it comes to depression. This particular emotional dis-ease can, does, and will hit all of us—not once, but repeatedly—and the more intelligent, creative, and progressive we are, the more susceptible we seem to be.

In an excellent book entitled *The Psychology of Jesus and Mental Health,* Raymond Cramer says, "Mental health is more than a science. It is an art. It is more than a body of fixed knowledge. It is a philosophy."[1] Or, what folks today call a life style. Dr. Cramer goes on to say, "In this art, through this philosophy, it is the individual who holds the key . . . each one has the capacity to be free—[but] he himself must strike the first blow."[2]

TAKE THE OFFENSIVE

You can strike a blow at endogenous depression by seeing your doctor, getting good medical help, and following it. Depression which has a physical cause is wonderfully responsive to certain pharmaceuticals available today. So let your family physician know how you feel. In a great many cases relief is available.

Exogenous depression responds more slowly, because the situation which caused it is not likely to change quickly. However (and this is very important), with the help of a caring person—professional or otherwise—you can work on your attitude toward the situation. With a change in attitude there is often a change in mood. By attacking the one thing under your control—your attitude—you can strike a blow for mental health.

With neurotic depression, the primary subject of this book, there are many blows you can and should strike. Not the least of these is to understand the causes—get hold of the spiritual principles designed to counteract those causes—and apply them.

GRASP THE CAUSES

Let's review where we've been so far. If there is a root cause for neurotic depression, it would appear to be perfectionism. When you fall prey to it, you deny your basic humanity. You forget you are dust and, like dust, are unstable—in a manner of speaking—highly susceptible to the winds of influence which blow upon you. Perfectionism sets you up for inevitable failure, because there's no way you can meet its unrealistic demands.

When you fail to measure up, you become vulnerable to a second anti-attitude: worthlessness. This often takes the form of chronic regret about past failures which have never been dealt with creatively in the love of God. There is a tendency to universalize your feeling of worthlessness just as you universalized the demand of perfectionism. "If I'm not all right, I must be all wrong!" That isn't true, of course, but Satan will make you believe it if you let him.

Then, in an effort to assuage this feeling of worthlessness, you get actively involved in an effort to acquire those things which the world says make you a person of worth. You begin investing your total sense of worth in things which are vulnerable to loss. As a consequence your stress level goes higher and higher.

At this point, frayed and frazzled from the hassle of acquisitiveness, your normal need for pleasure as a healthy release from stress is perverted by Satan into hedonism. Pleasure for its own sake. Pleasure as the sole goal in life. This not only doesn't satisfy, it leaves you less and less satisfied. In the end it turns out to be dreadfully boring.

ENTER DEFENSIVENESS

Satan's fifth anti-attitude is a beaut! Recognizing every-thing is *not* "coming up roses" for you, the last thing you want is for others to recognize it, too. No one—*but no one*—is allowed to suggest you are less than you can be.

You become hard. Brittle. Tough. Aggression is increasingly apparent. As your anger turns inward, you tend to be increasingly unforgiving, intolerant, and critical. Charity, if there is any, is more often than not manipulative, an effort to get strokes for yourself. Rage is near the boiling point. This retroflexed anger either expresses itself in an aggressive way—defensiveness—or it results in withdrawal, a further retreat into depression.

RETROFLEXED ANGER AND DEPRESSION

To get on top of this you must understand neurotic depression is a form of self-punishment. It is caused, in part, by anger directed at yourself. Sometimes this anger is so intense you not only wish others would drop dead, you have a strong desire to accommodate the world by dropping dead yourself. While that thought delights the adversary, it grieves the heavenly Father. Yours is a happy God (1 Tim. 1:11). He is at work in you both for your good pleasure and his own (Phil. 2:13). The thought of your doing something to harm yourself grieves him deeply. Its cause? Retroflexed anger!

Retroflexed anger begins when—right or wrong—you become angry at someone or something. Instead of expressing your anger creatively and redemptively you attempt to bury it. But, like the proverbial cat with nine lives, anger refuses to roll over and play dead. If it is not directed outward in a healthy way, it is directed inward (retroflexed) upon yourself. In addition to causing physical difficulties, this unfortunate way of handling anger can create various kinds of emotional dis-ease including depression.

To beat it you must learn the comfort of confrontation. This means learning to forgive. It also means learning to be assertive in ways which enable you to be real and heal.

MERCY AS TOUGH LOVE

"Blessed are the merciful, for they shall receive mercy" (Matt. 5:7). That doesn't sound confrontive, does it? Examined more closely, however, mercy takes on the shape of tough love—very tough love—as the following paraphrase makes clear:

RX *for defensiveness: Happy are those for whom extending forgiveness becomes second nature—who are able to love their neighbor creatively, assertively and redemptively, because they do so from the perspective of healthy self-love. They will be given the privilege of being human, too.*

Being merciful is not an attitude or act which is only directed outward. It must also be directed inward. You must learn to be merciful to yourself. Tolerant with yourself. Accepting of yourself. You can accomplish this by changing the way you talk to yourself.

Jesus said: "Blessed are the poor in spirit, for theirs is the kingdom of heaven" (Matt. 5:3). Based on that, you need to tell yourself: "Hey, it's OK to be human. I'm going to permit myself to be imperfect, to experience all my feelings, and give myself room to grow."

Jesus said: "Blessed are those who mourn, for they shall be comforted" (Matt. 5:4). In the light of that you need to tell yourself: "I'm not going to wallow around in despair anymore. I faced a temptation. I failed to meet it constructively. I fell flat on my face. But I have accepted God's provision for failure of all kind. I'm going to get up and go on. I'm guilty, but forgiven—praise the Lord!"

Jesus said: "Blessed are the meek, for they shall be comforted" (5:5). Based on that, you need to tell yourself: "Hey, I'm not going to waste any more energy trying to prove I am a person of worth. I'm a child of God. I'm a King's kid. I've been redeemed. That alone gives me worth! I don't have to—and I won't—waste any energy trying to convince myself or others of that fact."

Jesus said: "Blessed are those who hunger and thirst for righteousness, for they shall be satisfied" (5:6). In the light of that, you need to tell yourself: "I have a God-given gift and capacity for pleasure. I'm not going to let Satan pervert it and turn it into hedonism. I'm going to break out of boredom. I'm going to harness this natural capacity and channel it for my good as well as that of others. I'm going to choose righteousness, right-wise-ness, so I can be consistent with my true self."

EXIT DEFENSIVENESS!

When you've come that far, you're ready for the next thing Jesus said: "Blessed are the merciful, for they shall receive mercy" (Matt. 5:7). Based on that you should tell yourself: "I'm going to reject Satan's fifth anti-attitude, defensiveness, because I don't have any need to be defensive anymore!"

Defensiveness is a symptom of inner unrest. An absence of peace. The presence of internal strife or conflict. J. B. Phillips translates James 4:1 to read: ". . . what about the feuds and struggles that exist among you—where do you suppose they come from? Can't you see that they arise from conflicting passions within yourselves?" But by taking prescription No. 5 seriously, you can say: "I'm going to reject Satan's lie; I'm not going to accept this anti-attitude of defensiveness. I have no need to be defensive. If God—who is absolutely holy—loves me, accepts me, and forgives me, who am I not to love, accept, and forgive myself!"

In other words, by serious and consistent application of God's grace, you are now able to operate from a position of strength—of healthy self-love—which allows you to admit it when you (inevitably) goof.

I love the story about an incident which happened

on opening night in a Chicago theater. There were two experienced actors and one neophyte. In the first act the inexperienced actor was to threaten one of the other actors with a gun, but not to shoot. The fatal shot wasn't due till the third act. In his excitement the neophyte pulled the trigger. The gun went off. The experienced actor did just what any good actor would do. He hit the floor. The third actor, trying to keep the play going, dropped to his knees, leaned over the "dead" man, pressed his ear to his heart, and said, "Maybe he isn't dead. Maybe it was just a glancing shot. Yes! I think I hear his heart beating." Looking up at the neophyte he said, "Here, listen and see if you can hear it beating, too." The young actor got down on his knees, listened for a full minute while the audience sat in silence, got up, and said distinctly, "Nope, he's deader than a mackerel!" After a hurried conference back stage, the curtain came down, the manager walked to the front and said calmly, "Due to a rare example of stupidity, we will now hear the first act again from the beginning."[3]

It's important, you see, to be strong enough and honest enough to admit it when you goof and start over. You must also be prepared to extend that privilege to others. If God—who is absolutely holy—loves your neighbor, accepts your neighbor, and forgives your neighbor, who are you not to love, accept, and forgive your neighbor! But to do that, you must first be able to be merciful with yourself.

When Jesus said, "Love your neighbor as yourself" (Matt. 19:19), he was giving more than a commandment. He was stating a principle: you will tend to think and feel about others as you think and feel about yourself. If you can learn to accept God's provision for failure of all kinds, then extending forgiveness will, in time, become second nature to you. You will be able to love your neighbor creatively, assertively, and redemptively, because you do so from the perspective of healthy self-love.

AMBIVALENCE IS NORMAL

At this point, you must face up to your mixed feelings toward others. Remember, you have freed yourself to feel all your feelings. This means sometimes you're going to have both positive/negative, like/dislike, love/hate feelings toward others. A third-grader wrote a note to the boy sitting in front of her. He'd given her a tough time on the playground at recess. "Dear Bobby: I hate you. Love, Mary." A healthy, quite realistic attitude!

A man woke up in a casket with a lily in his hands. As he lay there he got to thinking. "If I'm alive, what am I doing here? If I'm dead, why am I hungry?" We have these mixed feelings, you see, and it's important for you to realize that at the same time you may feel both alive and dead, positive and negative, like and dislike, love and hate toward another person.

"This concept is critical in understanding human or interpersonal relationships. Whenever two persons get close to each other they will learn more things to dislike about each other as well as things to like. The more intimacy the more ambivalence. In a sense we humans are like porcupines, the closer we get to one another the more it hurts. Mature persons know this and therefore don't expect either another person or relationship to be either totally good or totally bad. They know that the closer they get the more mixed the bag will be.

"But apparently some depressed persons haven't learned this in childhood. They tend to see people in black or white terms. They're unable to view people as complex and multifaceted. As a result they alternate between like and dislike of another person rather than entertain both feelings at the same time."[4]

Some of this may come from perfectionism projected onto others. The extreme demands you place on yourself are passed along to others. One thing is certain, however, *until you are able to deal with your anger toward another person, you cannot be merciful to that person. Anger is an unavoidable human response to many of life's situations. The question is, what do you do about it? How do you handle it?* The best way is by caring enough to confront the object of your anger. You do this in three stages.

LOVE CREATIVELY

To love creatively means to recognize, admit, and feel your anger—attempt to identify its source—and through creative responses reverse or correct the cause.

Often anger is rooted in what psychologists call "injunctions" which come from parents, older brothers and sisters, school and church officials, the society in which you live. Among these injunctions are such messages as: "Don't be angry." "Be nice." "Be sweet." Translated that means: "Be perfect!"

As a young child your brain was very fertile. These powerful messages (injunctions) were "taped," so to speak, in your brain. After a time, by force of repetition, they became a significant part of you. As a consequence, even though you are separated by death or distance from the authority figures of your childhood, there may be times when you can still hear them say: "Don't be angry." "Be nice." "Be sweet." "Be perfect!"

In childhood, ignoring these injunctions usually implied a penalty. Sometimes it came as an aggressive action—a slap across the mouth—if you expressed anger. Sometimes it came in the form of rejection—the other person withdrew from you or sent you away from them— if you became annoyed. These penalties fostered inhibition. Hence when anger comes, you suppress it thinking: "I shouldn't feel this way—but I do! Something must be wrong with me. If anyone knew how I really feel—ouch!" Caught in a double bind you begin to "gunnysack."

I learned that term from Juan Aguila, a licensed

marriage and family counselor serving on our staff. Juan would ask you to picture yourself carrying a gunnysack over your shoulder. All the hurts and feelings you're hesitant to express go into the gunnysack.

An anger-producing situation arises. The "injunction tape" from your childhood plays, "Don't be angry. Be sweet. Be kind." In other words deny your true feelings. So you choke back the anger and stuff it into your gunnysack.

After awhile this becomes habitual. Anger develops. Your childhood "injunction tape" plays "don't feel that way." You deny your feelings. You stick them in your gunnysack and play the "phony" game.

If the tape plays "be perfect"—that is, don't make *any* mistakes—you start walking on eggs. Now you're dumping feeling after feeling into your gunnysack. The pressure mounts. However, like the proverbial cat, anger will not roll over and play dead. Finally, you explode. So it's important that you learn to live creatively—to care enough to confront positively and lovingly the cause of your anger. It may produce a bit of hurt. But, better a little hurt now, than an explosion and big hurt later.

RETAPE CERTAIN MESSAGES

One way you can learn to love creatively is by "retaping" certain messages. There is no way to erase bad messages, because your brain is a computer with a fail-safe system which won't let you forget. But there's ample room for other messages.

So when you get the "be perfect" message—a nice mommy, daddy, or preacher injunction!—ask yourself, "Is that the right message? Is that realistic?" Obviously, the answer is "no." Whether it came from mother, father, or preacher!

Next, say to yourself, "I'm incapable of being perfect. Therefore, I give myself permission to be imperfect. To experience all my feelings. To grow." Do this in other areas where injunctions coupled with implied penalties have created inhibitions. In time—by force of repetition—you can reprogram yourself to love creatively.

LOVE ASSERTIVELY

It's more difficult to love assertively, but it can be done! Begin by learning to discharge your anger. Anger is an energy that doesn't just evaporate. If it isn't discharged in a positive way, it will turn back (retroflex) on you. So you need to find creative ways to be assertive and in the process discharge your anger.

PLAY HARD

One way is to play. Think about the more active games available to you. Tennis. Racket ball. Handball. Golf. What do they involve? Hitting something! Jogging, bike riding, walking are less "aggressive," but they, too, are actions which allow you to discharge anger energy.

WORK HARD

Another way to do it is by working in the right way. I called one of our staff members this week. When he came to the phone, he said, "I've been practicing what you preach."

"That's good to hear," I replied.

"Yep," he continued, "I was pulling weeds—getting rid of that overstress you've been talking about." Terrific, I thought. I ought to do the same. Instead, I lay down till the impulse went away!

You can also learn to love assertively through certain learned psychotherapy activities such as screaming. Now, be careful when and where you do that! I was talking to a gal the other day who has been struggling with depression caused by some unresolved feelings toward her father. "When my 'gunnysack' gets too full, I climb into my car, go for a drive with the windows rolled up, and scream. It feels great!"

If you don't want to do that, try sighing. Take a deep breath, get your lungs and diaphragm full, then let it out—all out! You'll be surprised how a half dozen deep sighs will help release tension. Your facial muscles can get terribly tense when you "gunnysack." A sigh or deep breath can relax them. Your hands, arms, neck, and shoulder muscles also grow tense when feelings are suppressed.

Perhaps you've observed people going through "rituals of anger." One of the most common is the way they drive. They're potential killers! It may be their spouse, boss, or customer they want to kill. But behind that wheel, every angry feeling they haven't handled creatively is being expressed in an uncreative way.

Then, too, your heart and other "innards," your back, legs, and feet pay a price when you "gunnysack." Jogging, walking, hiking are all wonderful ways to deal with pent-up anger and allow emotional discharge to occur.

SOME BIBLICAL EXAMPLES OF ASSERTIVE LOVE

Maybe you're feeling "un-Christian" about learning to love assertively. What did Jesus do when he found the moneychangers in the temple? Wham! Over went the tables. Bam! Out went the stuff merchants were using to defile God's temple. Jesus asserted himself! In a physical way he discharged his anger. What did Moses do when he came down from the mountain and saw the people worshiping their handmade gods? He smashed the tablets God had written by hand! God didn't zap him. So don't be afraid to love assertively. If you need some help in learning how to do this, there are Christian counselors all over the country who can teach you how to assert yourself creatively and discharge your anger therapeutically through physical activity.

PRAY HARD

I know that sounds religious. But praying hard is extremely helpful. Honest! I know from experience. I've been in situations where I couldn't chop wood. Dig weeds. Or hit a ball. I couldn't play. I couldn't do physical work. So I prayed. Hard. Out loud. So my ears would hear what my mouth was saying and I'd know what I meant! "God, I have this feeling. I don't like it—but I admit it. I'm incapable of loving assertively right now, so I give my anger to you. I dump it into the ocean of your love." Then, as creative thoughts come, I would write down ways I could love assertively when the time was right.

In our premarital counseling program we use a cassette album which over a period of several weeks requires the couple to spend approximately twenty-four hours together in active listening.[5] Filling out response sheets. Sharing and discussing their answers. They probably engage in more real communication with each other than many married couples do in twenty-four years! Among other things, we teach them how to deal with irritations.

One day, during a follow-up session scheduled with a couple after they had listened to the tapes and completed the workbooks, I asked the young gal, "How do you do it? How do you deal with irritations?"

"The first thing I do is ask myself, is it really important? There are things that irritate me about other people, but if I had to choose between the person with the irritation or not having the person at all the choice would be simple. So, if it isn't important I forget it." I believe it was William James who said: "The art of being wise is the art of knowing what to overlook." Obviously, at age twenty-three this young lady had already gained a good deal of wisdom!

She continued, "If it is important, I pray about it and ask God to help me change my attitude." Beautiful! Many things are important or unimportant, depending on how you look at them. Like the guy who, when the doctor walked into his hospital room one morning and said, "Your cough sounds better today." The man replied, "It should, I practiced it all night!"

On the other hand, there was that sweet little third-grader who greeted her daddy at the door one evening excitedly, "Daddy! Daddy! I almost hit a home run today."

"You did? Wonderful! Tell me about it."

"Well," she said, "I swung at the ball, hit it, it almost reached the pitcher, who threw it to the first baseman. She dropped it, and I ran to second base. The second baseman dropped it, and I ran to third base. The third baseman dropped it and I headed for home plate. If they had dropped the ball one more time, I would have hit a home run!"

Having a positive attitude toward life's situations really helps. So the second step in my young friend's formula for coping with irritation was, "I pray about my attitude and ask God to help me change it." There are four billion people in this world. You don't have to be a genius to realize it's easier to change your attitude than it is to change 3,999,999,999 other people!

"Then," she said, and this was beautiful, "if it still continues, I ask the Lord to show me how to lovingly confront the cause of the irritation and invite that person to participate with me in finding a solution."

Pretty good stuff, don't you think! At twenty-three she had already learned you need to ask permisson to have a confrontation. If you're going to have a clean fight, you really have to ask permission of the person with whom you want to fight.

But first of all, pray. Write down how you're going to do it. Exhale two or three times. Be aware of your body language and body position. These can "say" so much in times like this. Make sure you're face to face and have real eye contact. Allow space in the conversation. Think before you speak. Practice what's called active listening. Make every attempt to understand the feelings of the other person. By verbal and nonverbal means let the person *know* you understand—or at least want to!

Next, use "I" messages. "You" messages are accusative. They are tantamount to pointing a finger of accusation at the other person. They tend to put the other person down. "I" messages express how *you* feel: "I'm talking about myself now. I accept responsibility for what I'm about to say. I may not be right, but this is how I feel."

Think before you speak, but speak! Be assertive. Be selective in words you use. Eliminate imperatives: "You ought to." "You should." "You must." They come off as commands—injunctions—which make the other person defensive. Remember: if your response is defensive, you will make the other person defensive.

LOVE REDEMPTIVELY

When you love redemptively you say to another person, "You're important enough to me for me to risk being assertive." And it is a risk! When you first try it, Satan will attack you from all sides. He'll start playing all those "childhood injunction tapes." And it won't be easy to switch channels. But you can do it. You can learn to say, "It's OK to be human. It's OK to feel all my feelings. Feelings have no morality. They just are. I'm willing to take the risk—to love redemptively."

As a consequence, you'll be real and heal. By opening the lines of communication and keeping them open, honesty will become the basis of your relationships. You won't have to guess any more (and we're all lousy guessers!). You'll know where you stand. Your neighbor will know where he or she stands. Without being aggressive and rude—the main difference between assertion and aggression is that assertion never puts the other person down, it never takes the form of an assault on the other person's character—you'll enjoy the comfort of confrontation. You'll be real and heal. You'll heal yourself. You'll heal your neighbor. And you'll heal your little corner of the world. If I make it sound easy—it isn't. But it's well worth the effort. Try it and see!

8

PUT IT ALL TOGETHER

Happy are the utterly sincere, for they will see God!
Matthew 5:8

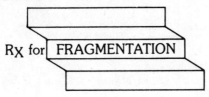

Rx for FRAGMENTATION

A vacationer to the rugged northern California coast stopped to watch a famous artist at his work. After awhile the kibitzer leaned over the shoulder of the famed painter and, with the superficiality all too common of sightseers, said, "Sir, I can't see any such light and color in this scene as you're putting on your canvas." To which the artist replied, "Oh, but don't you wish you could."

Have you had moments when you couldn't see the light and color and beauty and brightness of life? I have. Maybe you're feeling that way right now. Your memory bank assures you the loveliness is there, but your eyes can't see it. Because one of the curses of even mild depression is an inability to see life clearly.

Your happy God wants you to be healthy, whole, and happy too. Satan's desire for you is the exact opposite.

So for every Beatitude which directs you upward into happiness, the adversary has an anti-attitude which drags you downward into depression.

UPWARD INTO HAPPINESS

This graphic may help you understand the dynamics of what God wants to do for you.

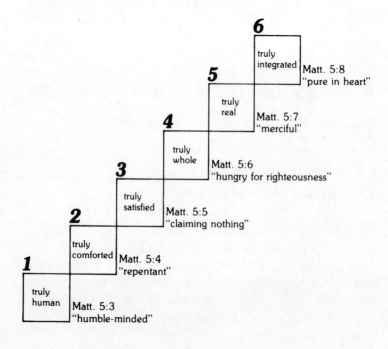

6
truly integrated — Matt. 5:8 "pure in heart"

5
truly real — Matt. 5:7 "merciful"

4
truly whole — Matt. 5:6 "hungry for righteousness"

3
truly satisfied — Matt. 5:5 "claiming nothing"

2
truly comforted — Matt. 5:4 "repentant"

1
truly human — Matt. 5:3 "humble-minded"

Square one is Christ's invitation to be truly human. You learn this by discovering what it means to be humble-minded (Matt. 5:3).

Square two refers to being truly comforted. This happens when you're really sorry for sin (Matt. 5:4).

Square three offers the possibility of being truly satisfied. By claiming nothing, God gives you this good earth with full freedom to enjoy it (Matt. 5:5).

Square four promises you can be truly whole. Righteousness, right-wise-ness, synchronizes your entire being by putting you in touch with your true self (Matt. 5:6).

Square five invites you to be truly real. Loving creatively, assertively and redemptively produces healing for yourself and others (Matt. 5:7).

This leads to square six and the assurance of being truly integrated. The utterly sincere—J. B. Phillips' phrase for the pure in heart—are blessed people, as the following paraphrase makes plain:

RX *for fragmentation: Happy are those who are undivided (integrated)—who are in touch with their feelings, goals, and desires and accept responsibility for themselves when they are less than whole. They will know that God accepts them.*

The previous graphic depicted what God wants to do for you. Below is one showing how the adversary tries to counter God's blessings. While the Beatitudes are clear, Satan's anti-attitudes are equally clear.

Opposite truly human he puts perfectionism—the idea you must be superhuman.

Opposite truly comforted he puts worthlessness—the rejection of any hope you can be better than you are.

Opposite truly satisfied he puts acquisitiveness—the frantic effort to secure those things the world says makes you a person of worth.

Opposite truly whole he puts hedonism—pleasure run amuck.

Opposite truly real he puts defensiveness. With "dukes" up, you resent the suggestion it might not be well with your soul.

The result is the opposite of true integration: fragmentation. A state of soul in which you are divided within yourself. Out of touch with your true thoughts, feelings, and desires, you become a taker. A user.

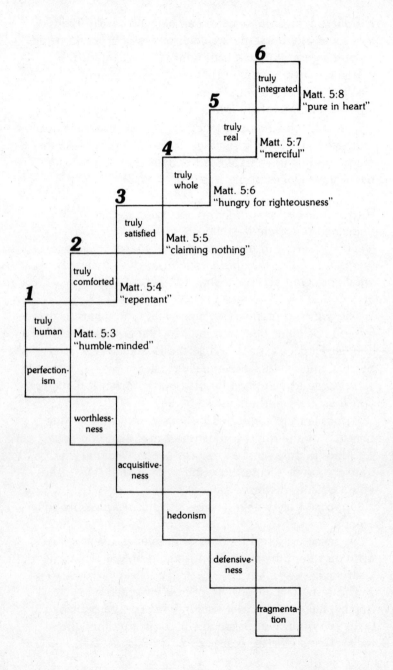

6 truly integrated — Matt. 5:8 "pure in heart"

5 truly real — Matt. 5:7 "merciful"

4 truly whole — Matt. 5:6 "hungry for righteousness"

3 truly satisfied — Matt. 5:5 "claiming nothing"

2 truly comforted — Matt. 5:4 "repentant"

1 truly human — Matt. 5:3 "humble-minded"

perfection-ism

worthless-ness

acquisitive-ness

hedonism

defensive-ness

fragmenta-tion

Unwilling or unable to accept responsibility for what you have become or are becoming, your life is characterized by restless and resentful discontent.

FRAGMENTATION AS DEPENDENCY

Roger Barrett provides a dozen or so symptoms of fragmentation in the form of dependency.[1] Among them is reliance on others. The fragmented person tends to be "other" directed. Unable to experience self-acceptance he or she looks to others for approval. This results in a precarious way of living. Other people can't be controlled. Hence there is the constant fear of losing this source of support. The thought he or she may not be available when needed is both scary and depressing.

Dependency also expresses itself in an inordinate need for affirmation and affection. The fragmented person becomes a love junky always looking for another fix. Relationships are based on need, not love. While love and need are a lot alike, they are not the same. Hence the love junky is a candidate for depression when the person(s) he or she is depending on fails to provide the needed fix.

Then there are what Dr. Barrett calls "learned con games." These are designed to manipulate other people, and they take many shapes. Dominance. Weakness. Controlling. Withdrawing. Always needing to be right. Playing stupid. Becoming nonfunctional.

The inevitable result of dependency is that you begin to hate the person upon whom you have become dependent. You feel ambivalent. Indecisive. Confused. Like the little dog which wandered into the Los Angeles coliseum during a football game. About 80,000 people began to whistle all at once. The poor pup didn't know which way to turn—which whistle to respond to. The calls were coming from every direction. It wound up running around in circles. Similarly, some of the sad byproducts

of fragmentation are confusion, indecision, and loss
of direction.

GETTING TO SQUARE SIX

How do you get your act together? To begin with it's
important to understand it isn't God's standards which
set you up for the big letdown. It's Satan's anti-attitudes
which result in fragmentation. Being truly human leads
to being truly comforted, truly satisfied, truly whole, truly
real, and hence truly integrated—in touch with your true
feelings, goals, and desires.

Perfectionism, which is pride gone wrong, is the culprit.
"Pride goes before destruction, and a haughty spirit before
stumbling" (Prov. 16:18, NASB) and, as the graphic
shows, perfectionism leads to worthlessness, acquisitiveness, hedonism, defensiveness, and fragmentation.

So the answer to the big question of how you become
integrated is by being ready, willing, and able to go back
ever so quickly—*and as often as needed*—to square one.
Review what it means to be truly human. Remind yourself
you have freed yourself to feel all your feelings, have
accepted your imperfections, and given yourself
permission to grow.

Then, almost automatically, move on to square two.
Reaffirm God's provision for failure of all kind (confession,
repentance, and forgiveness) and rejoice in the fact you
are guilty, but forgiven—praise the Lord!

From there pass to square three. Relinquish any false
goals which may have temporarily captured your
attention. Retreat from any wrong turns you may have
taken in terms of priorities and values.

Then on through square four where you renew your
commitment to the objective of righteousness as a life
style, to square five where, once again, you forgive
yourself and others because God has forgiven you.

When all the above has happened habitually and repeatedly—*as often as needed, fifty times a day if necessary*—then, as the prescription for fragmentation says, you will be in touch with your feelings, goals, and desires. You will be integrated. Undivided. Truly together. And, by accepting responsibility for yourself each time you are less than whole, you get in tune with God. You see him. That is to say, you experience the reality of his life in your life—now! He ceases to be an impersonal idea and becomes One who is with you and for you because he loves and accepts you. The only response to that discovery is: wow! (Would you believe: hallelujah!)

UP THE DOWN STAIRCASE

Now, again, I'm not suggesting you become wonder woman or superman. I got a chuckle out of a blurb in the *Reader's Digest*. A pastor who had been making hospital calls stopped by the church office to pick up any last minute messages before going home. As he walked through the door he was stopped cold by a sign the janitor had placed in front of the floor he had just washed: "PLEASE DON'T WALK ON THE WATER."

I'm not trying to teach you how to walk on water. Nor am I offering easy answers to depression. It's far too complex a problem for that. What I am suggesting is a way to climb up the down staircase so you can move, however tentatively, from depression toward joy.

This may mean learning what to do when you blow it. All of us sin. All of us stub our toes and fall flat on our faces at times. I'm suggesting being flat on your face is an excellent posture for prayer! The real value in prayer is not in what it can give you, but in what it can make you. At its best, prayer is not so much a method of getting, as it is a means of growing!

RATIONALIZE, PENALIZE, OR GO THROUGH THE SQUARES?

There are three things you can do when you sin.
One—you can rationalize it. You can say such things as "everybody's doing it, therefore it's OK." To do so is to harm yourself, because you eliminate the desirable level of stress needed to move you forward toward the worthy goal of right-wise-ness.

Two—you can penalize yourself for sinning. Through neurotic self-punishment you can continue to condemn yourself and make yourself sick physically, emotionally, and spiritually. As mentioned before, there is a place for godly sorrow which leads to repentance. But once you have turned away from sin and headed in the other direction, there is no place for continuing regret. If you continue to condemn yourself for what should be seen as a momentary relapse, it becomes a preoccupation. This is not only unhealthy and un-Christian, it is absolutely unnecessary!

Three—you can "go through the squares"—*as often as needed, fifty times a day if necessary*—and thus discover what it means to be clean clear through. When you do, several things happen—all of them good! You reaffirm that you're truly human, truly comforted, truly satisfied, truly whole, truly real, truly integrated. You have the deep security of knowing you are integrated, undivided, and what is more, energized by the power of God to get on with the joy of living.

When Jesus talked about being pure in heart, he wasn't talking about perfectionism. If so, there wouldn't be any hope for any of us. None of us is capable of sinless perfection. Nor was he calling you to a prim, proper, pious, uptight attitude toward life. Jesus was the only genuinely free spirit who ever lived. And he said, "I am the way, and the truth, and the life" (John 14:6). I like to think of him saying: I am the way, walk me. I am the truth, know me. I am the life, live me. And if you walk my way, know my truth, and live my life, you'll be free too.

When Jesus called you to be pure in heart, he wasn't demanding that you enter into a kind of neuter morality akin to that of the angels who don't know what it is to fall flat on their faces. *He was expressing his concern, not so much for what you do, but for what you are: a child of God!*

It may be painfully obvious to you there are times when you're a wayward child. But the glorious message of the Christian faith is that God is more concerned about *you* than he is about what you *do!* Jesus knows you can't be the person you are meant to be if you are divided within yourself. So he invites you to be pure in heart. To be together. Integrated. Undivided. A famous theologian once told a group of students this sixth Beatitude should be translated: "Happy are those who are not double-minded, for they shall be admitted to the intimate presence of God." Right on!

What Jesus is asking for here has to do with your attitude as well as your behavior. "Pure" as Jesus used it means much more than "clean." Being clean is part of it, but it also means "solid" as when we speak of an object as being pure gold. We don't mean it is clean gold. We mean it is solid gold. It is free of any diluting alloy, and that's the sense of what Jesus is asking when he calls you to be pure in heart. He means to be undivided—to be free from any diluting alloy.

He is describing the direct antithesis of the double-minded, half-hearted, chameleon-like attitude of many Christians today. He's calling you to a life which is free of duplicity, insincerity, and instability. The pure in heart are not simple-minded people. They are single-minded people. Solid people. What psychologists call "grounded people." Their roots are firmly set in the good, nourishing soil of God's love and acceptance. They are undivided. They are integrated. They are in touch with their true feelings, goals and desires. As a result, they are ready to accept responsibility for themselves, when they are less than whole.

I'm continually amazed at the fascinating new computers coming out these days. They're almost human. A publication put out by the IBM Corporation reports— with tongue in cheek—computers are so human today, when one of them makes a mistake it will blame the mistake on another computer. Sounds terribly human, doesn't it?

But to be truly human is not a copout. It is not a way of shifting blame. It is not an escape from responsibility. To be truly human is to possess enough strength of char- acter to admit your imperfections, give yourself permission to grow, and thus accept responsibility for yourself during momentary relapses when you're less than whole.

J. Wallace Hamilton was a wonderful preacher. When he was alive thousands of people listened to him every Sunday. He has been quoted as saying: "There are only two kinds of religion—magical and moral. One looks to God to do things for us, the other looks to him to do things in us and through us. Put this down and remember it. There is no disposition in Christ to leave men helpless, infantile and undeveloped, and to do for them what they must do within themselves. Magical religion does not make people good. It may excite their wonder, but it does not change their hearts or make them better . . . perhaps the worst punishment God could visit upon us would be to answer all our prayers, to break through by miraculous intervention (all the time), heal all our diseases, solve all our problems and leave us children, undeveloped (forever)."[2]

Jesus has no intention of doing that. He's not about to leave you helpless, infantile and undeveloped. He's calling you to be pure in heart. To be integrated. To be in touch with your feelings, goals, and desires. But he is also calling you to accept responsibility for yourself and what you are becoming or have become. When that happens you see God. That is, you know that God accepts you.

The Quest for the Holy Grail is a story about the cup

which was supposed to have been used during the Last Supper.[3] According to the legend it was in the Holy Grail that Joseph of Arimathea caught the last drop of blood which fell from our Lord's side as he died on the cross. Sir Galahad, along with the other knights of the Round Table, set out in quest of the Holy Grail. They find it, but to each it is different, because each sees it as a mirror of his own soul. To some of the knights it is cloaked in mystery because their hearts are fogbound with self-centeredness. To Sir Lancelot it is covered with holy wrath and fire because his heart is sinful. To Sir Galahad it is a vision of polished radiance, for his heart is pure. He has it all together. He is healthy, happy, and whole.

This is a parable of the different ways you may see God. There may be times when he is cloaked in mystery because your heart is full of self-centeredness. There may be times when you perceive him as a fearful judge because your heart is full of sin. When you see him in these ways, you are reflecting the immediate condition of your own soul.

But when you are pure in heart, when you are together, when you are integrated, when you are solid and grounded in obedience to him—not as a means of gaining merit but as a means of saying thanks for the merit you already have in Christ—then you see him as he is. You know that he accepts you.

That's why it's necessary to be born again. That's why those of us who are born again need to be filled with the Holy Spirit. We need to be controlled, dominated, and directed by the spirit of wholeness (holiness) because our hearts can alienate us from God. They can separate us from the source of all joy. Knowing that, the Psalmist cried, "Create in me a clean heart, O God, and renew a steadfast spirit within me" (Psa. 51:10, NASB).

Do you remember the story of Mary Magdalene? It isn't a pretty story. According to tradition she was a woman of the streets. A pawn in the hands of lustful men. In her loneliness she was more often sinned against than sinning.

One day she came in contact with Jesus, the purest of the pure. When he spoke to her he didn't condone her. But he didn't condemn her either! That day Mary Magdalene got up out of the dust of the road where she had lain, squared her shoulders, lifted her head, and for the first time in years looked people in the eye without shame. She knew her sins were forgiven and her heart was pure because she had seen God.

There were other people who saw Jesus that day, but they didn't see him as God. They looked at him through the eyes of their body. They observed his actions. And while they were impressed by what they saw, they didn't see him as God. Mary Magdalene did, because she saw him through the eyes of her heart. From that moment on she was never the same.

If Jesus could do that for a tawdry woman of the street, he can do it for you. All he asks is that you give him your heart—that you let him make it pure. Undivided. Unfettered by sin. A heart ready to taste and see that the Lord is good. Let him begin in you!

9

RETREAT FROM BITTERNESS

*Happy are those who make peace, for they will be known
as sons of God!* Matthew 5:9

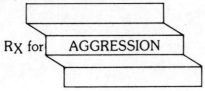

Rx for | AGGRESSION

There are two forms of aggression: active and passive.
Active aggression seeks to dominate a relationship. A
suitable symbol would be the bully who, in an abrasive
manner, moves against the object of his or her anger in
an attitude of "I'm OK. You're *not* OK!" By blaming
and attacking, he or she attempts to dictate the terms of a
relationship.

Passive aggression assumes the shape of submissive-
ness. Symbolized by the turtle who draws inside its shell,
this person moves away from the object of aggression in
an attitude of "I'm *not* OK, but *you're* not OK either!" By
pleasing and placating—a very subtle, calculating form of
manipulation—the passive aggressor attempts to control a
relationship.

Both forms of aggression are, as you can see, a retreat

into bitterness. When passive, you cancel yourself through a psychology of nonesteem: "*I'm* not OK." When active, you cancel out the other person through a psychology of destructiveness: "*You're* not OK." In either case the result is bad—all bad.

BITTERNESS: GUESS WHO'S THE REAL VICTIM

Bitterness is the result of accumulated anger which has not been dealt with creatively, assertively, and redemptively as we discussed in chapter seven. I'm convinced there are few attitudes more destructive personally or disruptive relationally than bitterness.

Dr. E. S. McMillen in his very practical book, *None of These Diseases*, rightly said: "What a person eats is not as important as the bitter spirit, the hates, and the feelings of guilt that eat at him. A dose of baking soda in the stomach will never reach these acids that destroy body . . . soul (and spirit)."[1] Bitterness is a poison which must not be allowed to remain in your system, because everyone is its victim.

It harms others, of course, and has a devastating effect upon relationships. Bitterness stings and hurts. It violates the law of love. It leads to contemptuous accusations and heartless repudiations. It puts you into "a cocoon of (your) own spinning" which so blinds you to the image of God in others you run roughshod over their feelings and desires.[2]

A lively five-year-old was being harshly scolded by his mother. Finally, having had all he could take, he looked her square in the eye and said, "I didn't come all the way down here from heaven to be yelled at!" Neither did the rest of us! There are better ways to spend life than being the object of other people's aggression.

However, while bitterness destroys the relationships with others, its real victim is you. Bitterness makes you narrow. Mean. Small. It shuts others out of your life and cuts you off from them and their friendship. It damages you emotionally, physically, and spiritually as you wallow around in self-pity, resentment, and unhappiness.

E. Stanley Jones pointed out on one occasion that a rattlesnake, if cornered, becomes so angry it will bite itself. That's exactly what bitterness is: a biting of yourself. You may think you are harming others, but the deepest harm is to yourself.

No wonder Jesus said: "Blessed [happy, fortunate, to be envied] are the peacemakers, for they shall be called sons of God" (Matt. 5:9, NASB). Or, as our paraphrase has it:

RX *for aggression: Happy are those who are always ready to initiate peace — who have the strength to lovingly confront, the willingness to reestablish broken relationships and the maturity to leave the response up to the other guy. They will be recognizably Christian.*

HOW TO BECOME A PEACEMAKER

How do you do that? By getting solid at the center yourself. A wife was overheard saying to her husband, "You're sure hard to live with." To which the man replied painfully, "*You* think I'm hard to live with. You ought to be *me!*" Pogo, the famous comic strip character, was made to say on one occasion, "We have met the enemy and it is us!"

"Scientists at Western Michigan University have discovered that the aggression of many species of animals is an instantaneous reaction to pain. A rat which has received a shock will instantly turn to attack another rat if one is near. Pain will even cause an animal to attack a member of a different species, including species which it normally avoids. A raccoon, for instance, will attack a rat which had nothing to do with its experience of pain. If it can't find another animal, the hurt animal will attack anything—even a stuffed toy."[3] Does that suggest to you that one basic human need is to get rid of the pain inside (which results in attacks and accusations against others) by making peace with God and yourself?

The peace Jesus is talking about in Matthew 5:9 is not the absence of disturbance. It is an armistice within your own soul—the end to the civil war raging within you, a unifying of the conflicting desires and ambitions which have created strife and turmoil.

Until you are at peace with yourself there will be no peace in your relationships. As long as you are at odds with yourself you will be at odds with others.

Hence, you must be born again. You must deal with the source of the pain inside you—the root of *all* aggression—sin! Then, when born again, you must be filled with the Holy Spirit. People in the Bible were "filled" with many things: anger, fear, greed, etc. In the terminology of Scripture they were controlled by anger, fear, greed, etc. Thus to "be filled with the Spirit" (Eph. 5:18) is not an emotional, but volitional matter. It will find expression in your emotions, but it centers in your will. At the bottom line is a choice on your part to be dominated, directed, *controlled* by love, integrity, and wholeness.

When you get solid at the center, you can begin to express that solidarity at the circumference of life in the relationships you share. Having made peace with God and yourself, you are free to become a peacemaker. You are able to initiate peace with others. To move from introversion to extroversion. From self-centeredness to multi-centeredness. From preoccupation with yourself to genuine interest in others.

In *The Secret of Happiness*,[4] Billy Graham asks us to visualize a right angle triangle sitting on its horizontal base. At the apex or highest point of the triangle is God. At the point where the perpendicular line meets the base line is you. At the opposite end of the horizontal line are others. Billy says, "There, in geometric form, you have a visual diagram of our relationship with God and man . . . peace flows down from God and out to our fellow men. We become merely the conduit through which it flows."

This means peace is an active word. A dynamic word. A practical word. A hard-working, down-to-earth, real-life word. It is love reaching out at whatever cost or consequence to repair relationships sin has sundered.

CAN YOU TOP THIS?

One of the finest illustrations of retreat from bitterness occurred in the jungles of Ecuador. On January 8, 1956, five young missionaries were murdered by the Auca Indians. Among them were Nate Saint and Jim Elliott. Jim was survived by his widow, Elizabeth, Nate by his sister, Rachael. Though they had every reason to be bitter, the two women chose not to retreat into bitterness. Instead, they committed themselves with renewed fervor to language study, determined to finish the task Nate, Jim, and the three other young martyrs had begun.

The Missionary Aviation Fellowship, with which the five men were associated, continued making gift drops to the tribal people, attempting to communicate friendship. Months later Rachael and Betty arrived in Ecuador. They succeeded in establishing a relationship with the Aucas and began to communicate Christ's love to the men who had killed their brother and husband. One by one these so-called savages received Jesus. The payoff came several years later when the young son of Nate Saint was baptized in the same river near the very place his father had been martyred. The Auca pastor who baptized him was one of the men who had killed his dad!

Happy are those who are always ready to initiate peace. Who have the strength to lovingly confront, the willingness to reestablish broken relationships and the

maturity to leave the response up to the other guy.
They will be recognizably Christian.

START A POSITIVE CHAIN REACTION

What are the steps to take if you would retreat from
bitterness? Decide where you are on the down staircase
and begin there. One by one replace the anti-attitudes
of Satan with the Beatitudes of Jesus and move up the
down staircase.

It's fascinating to me that you can begin on any level
heading downward into depression—hedonism, fragmentation, acquisitiveness, etc. By being truly human,
granting others the same right, and going on from there,
you can reverse your direction. You will experience true
comfort, true satisfaction, and so on. The blessed attitudes
of Jesus are just what the doctor ordered as correctives
for broken relationships.

For the moment, let's assume retroflexed anger has put
you in a state of aggression. So start there. Choose to be
filled with the Holy Spirit, focus your prayer thoughts on
the objects of your anger and give to them the same
privilege God has given you: the right to be truly human.
To be imperfect. To feel all their feelings. The freedom
to grow into the person God wants them to be. "X"
out aggression!

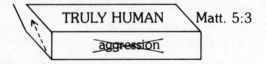

Then extend to them the same forgiveness God gave
you! Let the measure you received be the measure you
give. Through confession and repentance you were
cleansed and truly comforted. They can be, too. Guilty,
but forgiven—praise the Lord! "X" out fragmentation!

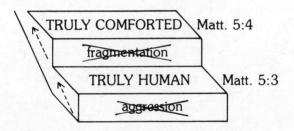

Third, take the pressure off them so they no longer need to perform up to your standards and expectations. Let them be God-tamed, God-trained, God-directed persons who claim nothing more than being pilgrims on a journey toward the objective of wholeness through Christ. "X" out defensiveness!

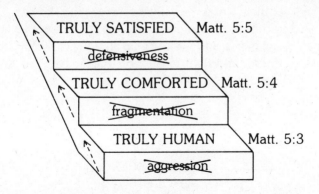

Now, there is no longer a need to act destructively. If God—who is absolutely holy—loves them, accepts them and forgives them, you can too.

Learning to use love as a verb and not a noun produces a complete change in your attitude. As a noun, love is a feeling. It seems to come out of nowhere and grab you. As a verb, love is an action. It doesn't grab you, you grab it. This means you can love anybody you choose to. By *willing* to love creatively and redemptively—by exercising love as a verb—you encourage others to be truly whole. "X" out hedonism!

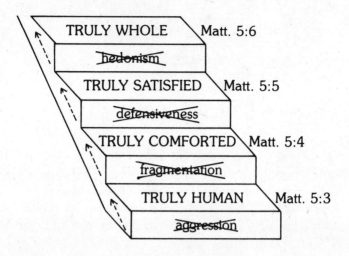

Then, let them know they are accepted. Instead of demanding that they change—that they acquire the ability to meet your needs and measure up to your expectation—grant them the right to their *own* feelings, goals and desires. By allowing them to be truly real it will become

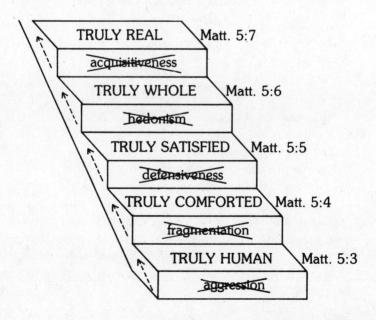

increasingly clear to them that *God* accepts them—
because *you* do! "X" out acquisitiveness!

Now things are really coming together. They are
becoming integrated persons and so are you. There's no
place for feelings of worthlessness. Chronic regret is
recognized as the negative force it really is. You and they
have a basic commitment to pleasing God—the only one
worth pleasing. "X" out worthlessness!

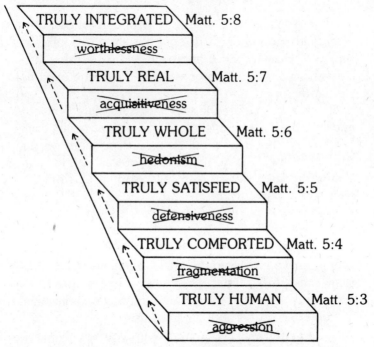

TRULY INTEGRATED   Matt. 5:8
worthlessness
TRULY REAL   Matt. 5:7
acquisitiveness
TRULY WHOLE   Matt. 5:6
hedonism
TRULY SATISFIED   Matt. 5:5
defensiveness
TRULY COMFORTED   Matt. 5:4
fragmentation
TRULY HUMAN   Matt. 5:3
aggression

Having reached a state of true acceptance and integrity
in your relationships you can be real and heal. David
Augsberger has a wonderful little book entitled *The Love
Fight—Caring Enough to Confront.*[5] He says, "I love
you. If I love you I must tell you the truth. I want your
love. I want your truth. Love me enough to tell the
truth." When a relationship has moved up the down
staircase to the point of acceptance and integrity, there
will be enough courage to confront.

"Care-fronting is the key to effective relationships. It's the way to communicate with impact and respect, with truth and love.

"'Speaking the truth in love'. . . is *the* way to mature right relationships shown us in Jesus.

"'Truthing-it-in-love,' the original phrase St. Paul chose, sums up the caring-confronting way of responding and respecting each other by taking the Jesus way *through* conflict.

"Care-fronting has a unique view of conflict . . . (it sees it as) neither good nor bad, right nor wrong. Conflict simply is. How we view, approach and work through our differences does—to a large extent—determine our whole life pattern. . . .

"Truth and love are the two necessary ingredients for any relationship with integrity. Love—because all positive relationships begin with friendship, appreciation, respect. And truth—because no relationship of trust can long grow from dishonesty, deceit, betrayal; it springs up from the solid stuff of integrity."[6]

A SELF-ADVERTISING KINSHIP

When you've moved through true humanity, true forgiveness, true satisfaction, true wholeness, true acceptance, and true integration, you have a relationship of true oneness. "X" out perfectionism!

You are at peace. With God. With yourself. With others. With the world. Peacemaking becomes natural for you—a life style. Jesus said: "Happy are those who go on making peace." The word he used in the Greek implies peacemaking is a life-long process.

When you are always ready to initiate peace (when you have the strength to lovingly confront, the willingness to reestablish broken relationships, and the maturity to leave the response to the other guy), you will be recognizably Christian. Your relationship to him will be self-advertising.

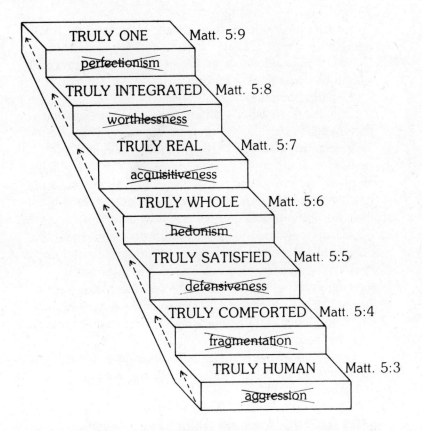

TRULY ONE	Matt. 5:9
~~perfectionism~~	
TRULY INTEGRATED	Matt. 5:8
~~worthlessness~~	
TRULY REAL	Matt. 5:7
~~acquisitiveness~~	
TRULY WHOLE	Matt. 5:6
~~hedonism~~	
TRULY SATISFIED	Matt. 5:5
~~defensiveness~~	
TRULY COMFORTED	Matt. 5:4
~~fragmentation~~	
TRULY HUMAN	Matt. 5:3
~~aggression~~	

Your attitudes and actions will mirror the qualities of your heavenly Father. There will be a close similarity between you. You'll be "a chip off the old block" so to speak. You'll be recognizably Christian and will bring honor to your Father's name.

MAKE IT A MOMENT TO REMEMBER

During a Biblelands Study Cruise I met a young woman who was obviously unhappy. She could find almost no reason to enjoy this marvelous experience. I learned she had been divorced. One day while ashore sightseeing with the group I fell in beside her and tried to draw her out.

"How long have you been divorced, Mary [not her real name]?"

"Well," she said, "as a matter of fact it's in process and will probably be finalized today."

"What happened?"

"The usual. Another woman. Only in this case it was my younger sister!"

I recognized she was hurting. Pointing to a little sidewalk cafe I said, "Let's have a cup of coffee and talk about it." It wasn't long before her anger, bitterness, and hate began to boil out. After awhile the group came by on their way back to the ship and we rejoined them.

Later that afternoon I got alone on deck and asked the Lord to show me how I could be of further help to her. And he said (not in an audible voice but in a manner I recognized to be his guidance), "John, the business isn't finished. It wasn't enough for her to come uncorked and get all that anger and ugliness out. She must complete the transaction and forgive her husband and sister." I continued praying, asking for wisdom as to how to approach her on this. When I looked up, who should be walking toward me but Mary. I called her over and said, "I've just been talking to the Lord about you. He told me to tell you the business we talked about this morning is unfinished. Among other things, you must forgive your husband and your sister."

"I know," she said quietly, "but I don't think I can."

"Mary, let me explain something about forgiveness. It isn't a feeling. It's an action. It's something you do."

I told her about Corrie ten Boom's beautiful illustration of the bell rope in a church steeple. To make the bell ring you begin tugging on the rope. At first there is no sound because sufficient momentum has not been built up. But once the bell has begun to ring all you have to do is keep your hand on the rope, give it a tug, and the bell will go on ringing. When you release the rope the bell goes on ringing for a while because momentum has been built up.

But if you keep your hand off the rope, the bell slows down and the ringing stops.

Bitterness, I pointed out, doesn't have much effect when it first begins. It takes awhile for the momentum of that emotion to build up. But once it gets to clanging away inside your soul, all you have to do to keep its clapper going is give an occasional tug. Release comes when you let go of the rope. When you decide to forgive. The bitter feeling may continue to clang away for a while, but if you keep your hand off the rope, ultimately it will grow still.

"Mary," I said, "I've found that whenever I want to do serious business with God, it works best if I can find a place where I will remember it. Then when the bad feelings and thoughts reoccur, I can use that place as a memory tool to recall and reaffirm a time when I did serious business with God. The middle of the Mediterranean would be an easy place to remember, don't you agree?"

"Yes."

"Would you like to go with me to the aft end of the ship and toss all that garbage inside you overboard?" She nodded.

We went down a couple of decks and made our way to the stern. She put her hand on the rail and I laid mine over hers to let her know she was not alone. "Do you want me to lead you in prayer?"

"No," she said.

"OK. Just make it an honest prayer, Mary. If you don't feel forgiving, tell the Lord that. Tell him exactly how you feel. He knows it anyway and understands. But also tell him what you decided to do today." We closed our eyes, bowed our heads, and she began to pray. It was a simple, beautiful, honest prayer. "God, I don't feel forgiving, but I know I must forgive. So now, as an act of the will, I forgive Bill and I forgive Betsy."

"How about yourself, Mary?"

"Yes, God. I forgive me, too." I prayed a short, agreeing prayer. The Bible says where two or more are agreed upon earth it shall be done in heaven (Matt. 18:19). So I agreed with her that forgiveness had been given as an act of the will.

We opened our eyes and to our amazement the sea was full of garbage! While we had been praying, the crew—several decks below—had been throwing the day's garbage overboard. It had spread across the wake of the ship as far as eye could see. "Mary, look! The sea is full of garbage! If you ever doubted God's love, never doubt it again. Through the miracle of precise timing he has given you a visual aid you can never forget." With a smile which was soul-deep she said softly, "I know. I know."

A month or two later I received a letter from her. "Today, Dr. John, on this beautiful Sunday morning . . . it came to me." (She had shared the anguish she'd been going through and was on the last page of her letter.) "God has a plan for me! I'm not going to lie down and die! I'm not going to go crazy. My mind is a valued thing, and God is not finished with it or me yet!

"Good grief! I didn't mean to ramble on and on. You're the one person I wanted to share this with, since, in a way, standing at the back of the ship 'throwing out the garbage' was . . . a turning point. I'll always remember it."

Following the cruise I flew to Holland where I was to speak for two weeks. I selected various aspects of forgiveness as my theme. One morning I told the folks at Rehoboth Springs where I was speaking, about the lady who stood at the aft end of the ship dumping her "garbage" overboard and the wonderful miracle of precise timing which happened out there in the middle of the Mediterranean Sea to affirm what she had done. A lady asked to see me and shared all her bitterness and hurt as the result of a broken home and incorrigible husband.

We talked about it and prayed about it. I did as much to help bring healing as time would allow. I returned to the States and a letter arrived from Holland about the same time Mary's did. My Dutch friend talked about her growing desire to minister to other singles. "Before I can do that I need to be helped first. I need to surrender all the bitterness. As I am writing, the Lord brings the moment at sea to my mind. I want to make this page the sea. Out of my pen is coming all of the bitterness and anger and hostility as I write it down upon this page. Will you—when you receive it—tear it up and throw it out. Perchance they will just come around for the garbage."

I did that for her at a Sunday morning service and invited the congregation to participate in the healing experience, too. Everyone was given a blank sheet of paper and was asked to write down things—those roots of bitterness—which were destroying relationships, perhaps even having a destructive effect physically, emotionally, and spiritually.

Then, as I did it for the lady in Holland, each person in the congregation tore up his or her paper. To get a feeling of mutual support we did it on the count of three. "One. Two. Three. . . ." The sound of paper ripping was glorious! "This we do, Father, in the dear name of Jesus Christ. Amen." Then the ushers came by with plastic garbage pails, the tiny shreds of paper were tossed inside, and our garbage was taken to the city dump where it was burned.

Why not do something similar? Take a blank sheet of paper. With pen or pencil write out all the bitterness, anger, and hurt inside. Maybe you'll need several sheets. That's OK. Is it a root bitterness toward your parents? Toward your children? Toward a brother or sister? Toward someone with whom or for whom you work? A neighbor? An in-law? Your spouse?

Joyce Landorf shares how she came to a moment when she had to forgive God.[7] That may sound ridiculous, but it isn't. And if you are holding feelings of bitterness against God because life isn't working out the way you think it should, or because you don't think he did a good job when he made you, get rid of that garbage right now. Write it on your piece of paper.

Now take your piece of paper and on the count of three, tear it into tiny pieces. Then dump it all in the garbage can. As you do pray a simple, honest prayer forgiving any and all toward whom you have been bitter. Remember: forgiveness isn't something you feel. It's something you do. For your sake. For his or her sake. And for Jesus' sake. Do it. Now!

HANG IN THERE

Happy are those who have suffered persecution for the cause of goodness, for the kingdom of Heaven is theirs!
Matthew 5:10

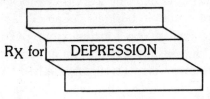

Rx for DEPRESSION

Joylessness in spite of everything is Satan's substitute for the joy God eagerly longs for you to experience in everything he allows. There are two profound principles here. First, God does not plan everything he allows, but, if you let him, he will overrule and use what he allows to achieve what he plans (Gen. 50:20; Rom. 8:28). Second, in those experiences he allows but does not plan he wants you to trust him to the point of being joyful and thankful—not *for* them, but *in* them—because, with your cooperation, he is committed to using them for good (Matt. 5:10, 11; 1 Thess. 5:18).

I'm convinced Jesus took such pains to give us a beautiful eight-part prescription for joy because he was aware of the kinds of tribulation born-again, Spirit-filled, growing Christians would face in this world (John 16:33).

Any believer who has ever taken God's Word and God's will and God's way seriously, has become a prime target for the enemy. With utter candor the Bible records how some of God's greatest servants have struggled with depression. Abraham. Isaac. Jacob. Joseph. Moses. Joshua. Almost all the judges. Saul. David. Solomon. And to name just a few of the prophets: Elijah, Jonah, Jeremiah. Such New Testament stalwarts as Peter and Paul were acquainted with this indigo mood.

Then, of course, there was Job—the textbook case of them all—a classic illustration of not one but all three major forms of depression. Think about his story for a moment and it will become clear he was victimized by exogenous depression—that which is external and situational—when everything of value to him was suddenly snatched away (Job 1:13-19). On the same day, like a bolt out of the blue, he lost his livestock (1:14, 15), his transportation business ("Camel Caravans, Inc.—We Hump to Please You") including the people who ran it (1:17), and, as if that were not enough, seven sons and three daughters died (1:19). All he had left was his wife and, for a while at least, she wasn't much of a prize (2:9).

To add insult to injury he was struck by endogenous depression—that which is internal and physical—when his body developed "sore boils from the sole of his foot to the crown of his head" (2:7, 8).

To top it off, he fell prey to neurotic depression—that which is internal and attitudinal—because, as the narrative so honestly reveals, his attitude toward life turned sour. He allowed resentment, self-pity, and bitterness to virtually consume him. "Afterward Job opened his mouth and cursed the day of his birth" (3:1). "Let the day perish on which I was born, and the night which said, 'a boy is conceived'" (3:3). "May that day be darkness . . ." (3:4). "As for that night, let darkness seize it . . ." (3:6). "Let

the stars of its twilight be darkened; let it wait for light
but have none, neither let it see the breaking dawn;
because it did not shut the opening of my mother's
womb, or hide trouble from my eyes. Why did I not
die at birth, come forth from the womb and expire?"
(3:9-11).

As if this oozing self-pity and resentment toward his life
situation were not enough, he also fell prey to bitterness:
"Therefore, I will *not* restrain my mouth; I will speak
in the anguish of my spirit, I will complain in the bitterness
of my soul" (7:11—italics mine).

It would take a full-blown, "hardhearted Hannah" not
to empathize with the feelings Job expresses. The point
we often miss, however, is that Job is *not* the culprit; *he
is the battlefield!* The first two chapters of Job set the
scene. "Now there was a day when the sons of God
came to present themselves before the Lord, Satan also
came among them" (1:6).

Parenthetically, I should explain the book of Job does
not give us a fully developed doctrine of Satan from the
Christian perspective. At this point, Satan, the archangel,
meets with the sons of God, lesser angels, in God's
presence. Not yet banished, Satan is "God's inspector of
man on earth." He is man's accuser, or prosecutor, so to
speak, before the Lord. When Jehovah asks him what
he's been doing, Satan explains he's been roaming about
the earth looking for a righteous[1] man (1:7). Jehovah
inquires, "Have you considered my servant Job? . . . a
blameless and upright man, fearing God and turning away
from evil" (1:8). Satan replies, "Of course, Job fears
God. Why shouldn't he! Look at all his blessings and your
protection which he enjoys. Remove that hedge with
which you have surrounded him. Let me take away his
blessings and I guarantee he'll 'curse you to your face'"
(1:9-11, author's paraphrase).

The Lord agrees to allow Satan to oppress Job, but
within limits: "All he *has*," not all he *is* (1:12). "Then

the Lord said to Satan, 'Behold, all that he has is in
your power, only do not put forth your hand on him.'"
This is crucial. Job is not the culprit. He is the battlefield.
The adversaries are God, who believes in Job, and Satan,
who does not believe in Job.

The whole human situation—including yours—is a
magnificent demonstration of the fact that God believes in
you even when you don't believe in him. He loves you
even when you don't love him. And he loves you enough
to let you be imperfect. To fail. To make mistakes and
fall. And when you do, if you let him, he picks you up,
dusts you off, gets you started on the right road again
and, most wonderful of all, walks that road with you.

KEEP THE BIG PICTURE IN MIND

To understand the implications of the eighth and last
Beatitude: "Blessed are those who have been persecuted
for the sake of righteousness, for theirs is the kingdom
of heaven. Blessed are you when *men* revile you, and
persecute you, and say all kinds of evil against you
falsely, on account of me" (Matt. 5:10, 11), it's important
to keep the big picture in mind. Be sure you understand
the *real* problem, because things are not always as they
seem on the surface.

A motorcyclist traveling across country was caught in a
driving rainstorm. It was bitterly cold. The zipper on his
jacket was broken. To make himself more comfortable he
stopped his bike, took off his jacket, and put it on
backwards so the solid back was in front to keep out the
cold. He zipped it up as far as he could, fired up his bike
and headed on down the highway. A short time later a
motorist, not seeing him, pulled out of a side road. The
cyclist, swerved to avoid the car, lost control, skidded
into a tree, and was knocked unconscious.

The driver of the car was chagrined to realize his
carelessness had caused this accident. He told the person

riding with him to call an ambulance and rushed over to the stricken cyclist to see if he could be of any help. When the ambulance arrived, the cyclist was dead. The highway patrol came and began to fill out an accident report. The driver of the car explained how he had not seen the motorcycle coming, had pulled out onto the highway, the cyclist had swerved to avoid him, lost control, skidded down the highway, and hit a tree. "I ran over to help him," the man continued. "When I got there I noticed his head was turned completely around and by the time I got it straightened up he was dead!"

Obviously, this fellow didn't understand the problem. And if you're going to cope successfully with depression, you've got to understand the nature of this dis-ease. When it comes to neurotic depression, at least, you must remember you're *not* the culprit, *you're the battlefield*.

"Satan hates the true Christian for several reasons. One is that God loves him, and whatever is loved by God is sure to be hated by the devil. Another is that the Christian, being a child of God, bears a family resemblance to the Father. . . . Satan's ancient jealousy has not abated nor his hatred for God diminished in the slightest. Whatever reminds him of God is without other reason the object of his malignant hate.

"A third reason is that a true Christian is a former slave who has escaped from the galley, and Satan cannot forgive him for this affront. A fourth reason is that a praying Christian is a constant threat to the stability of Satan's government. The Christian is a holy rebel loose in the world with access to the throne of God. Satan never knows from what direction the danger will come . . . such a danger is too great to tolerate, so Satan gets to the (born-again, growing Christian) as early as possible to prevent his becoming too formidable a foe. . . . The Spirit-filled life is not as many suppose, a life of peace and quiet pleasure. It is likely to be something quite the opposite.

"Viewed one way it is a pilgrimage through a robber-infested forest; viewed another, it is grim warfare with the devil. Always there is a struggle, and sometimes there is a pitched battle with our own nature where the lines are so confused it is all but impossible to locate the enemy or to tell which impulse is of the Spirit and which is of the flesh."[2]

Let it be understood then: you're not the culprit, you're the battlefield. But there's hope. Real hope. "Though we live in the world, we do not wage war as the world does. The weapons we fight with are not the weapons of the world. On the contrary, they have divine power to demolish strongholds. We demolish arguments and every pretention that sets itself up against the knowledge of God, and we take captive every thought to make it obedient to Christ" (2 Cor. 10:3-5, NIV).

With this provocative truth established (you're not the culprit, you're the battlefield), and this powerful statement of the spiritual resources available with which to fight Satan (2 Cor. 10:3-5), let me give you three big words which can help you successfully wage war against neurotic depression.

THE FIRST BIG WORD IS RESILIENCY

RX *for depression: Happy are those who are willing to be vulnerable as a part of the cost of experiencing righteousness (right-wise-ness)—who through praise put a positive, creative meaning on negative influences and thus are able to benefit from them. God's will—their highest good—will come to them in the now.*

The point I want to make in this paraphrase is that as a born-again, growing, Spirit-filled Christian, vulnerability to persecution "goes with the territory." It's part of the price you pay for being a "together" person.

I guess I've read the Beatitudes several thousand times.

Over the years I have probably referred to Matthew 5:10, 11 a hundred times in preaching situations. Yet it wasn't until I studied these verses in depth in preparation for this book that I really grasped what Jesus meant. Jesus is saying: when you make a commitment to right-wise-ness, that is, to the state of being right—really right—with God, yourself, and others, when you are committed to being in tune, it's inevitable that the sincerity of your commitment will be tested!

When you have this "hunger and thirst for righteousness" (5:6), Jesus says you can expect to be persecuted. For what? Yes! "For the sake of righteousness!" (Matt. 5:10). People who have it together intimidate those who don't. The whole make the nonwhole very uncomfortable. As a consequence, the integrated become the targets of the nonintegrated, beleaguered people about them.

It happens in the home. Even when the Christian spouse is filled with the Spirit, is especially sensitive and has gained some wisdom in how to model the life of Christ before his or her mate, the non-Christian spouse is intimidated by the Christian partner. The mere fact that the Christian exists—that he or she *is*—puts the spouse in touch with the reality of his or her nontogetherness.

I want to say something to those of my readers who are born-again, growing, Spirit-filled Christians married to unsaved or carnal mates: *Hang in there! You're OK. You're on the right track. And your commitment to right-wise-ness will pay off in the end.*

In a very special way our prescription is for you. Happy are those who are willing to be vulnerable as a part of experiencing righteousness. In the words of Jesus: "Great is your reward" (5:12, KJV).

LICKING DEPRESSION TAKES TIME

Hanging in there involves waiting. Most of us aren't too good at that. But time is a factor in God's cure for depression. Let me repeat that: *Time is a factor in God's cure for depression.* Waiting will not only renew your strength, it will also give God time to cause "all things to work together for good" (Rom. 8:28) as he promised to. What's more, it will help you get perspective.

NO EVENT IS FINAL

Nothing that ever happens can be properly appraised on the day it occurs. You must wait until all the days are in and their sum has been totaled up. In the meantime, however, you can wait "in hope" because as a Christian you know nothing comes to you which is not first filtered through God's love for you, so all irreversible harm is removed and what remains contains a blessing which could not otherwise be yours.

Remember Job. The Lord never gave *him* over to Satan, only those *things* which were his. Job's essential personhood continued to be hedged in by the heavenly Father. In the end all Job lost was restored with a bonus to boot. So, hang in there. As Bob Pierce, the intrepid missionary pioneer, once observed, 95 percent of the Christian's victory comes from just hanging on. If you want a Bible basis for it, claim Deuteronomy 33:25:' ". . . as thy days, so shall thy strength be" (KJV).

That doesn't mean you won't find periods of persecution to be depressing. But the very fact you're willing to be vulnerable—that you recognize it goes with the territory—hones in on the area of your attitude. By a change in attitude you're able to "get a leg up" on depression and in the process grow.

I believe it was Dale Carnegie who once pointed out that when manufacturers began to build automobile tires in large numbers, they tried to make a tire which would resist the abuse of the road. But it didn't work. Those old, solid, hard rubber tires were cut to pieces. So the manufacturers changed their attitude. They decided to make tires which would give a little. Which would absorb road abuse. Those tires are still with us. Why? Because they're resilient.[3]

The way to handle persecution "for the sake of righteousness"—which is inevitable—is not with resistance but with resilience. For resiliency can help you turn stumbling blocks into stepping stones.

A college lad was leading his younger sister up a mountain path. "It's no path at all," she complained. "It's all bumpy."

"Of course it is, Sis. But, don't you see, it's the bumps you're climbing on."

The same can be said of persecution "for the sake of righteousness." If you resent it, or rebel against it, or grudgingly resign yourself to it, there will be no profit in it for you. But if you take the right attitude toward it, it will lift your soul upward.

So don't try to bulldoze your way into joy. It won't work. Be like a stream. Learn to flow in, through, over, under, and around the obstacles to joy. Before you know it you'll be there.

THE SECOND BIG WORD IS RESOURCEFULNESS

Before I get into my next point, let me remind you in passing that Jesus did not say persecution is a proof of righteousness. As a matter of fact, the unpopularity you and I suffer at times may not be the result of our right-wise-ness, but our lack of it. Just because the whole world is arrayed against us is no proof we're suffering for the sake of righteousness.

Christ's prescription for joy (Matt. 5:10-12) does not apply to the resentment *we* arouse through a bad disposition. Or offensive manners. Or prudish criticism. Or pious misjudgments of others. And before you place the blame for any oppression you may be suffering upon your Christianity, submit yourself to an examination by the Holy Spirit to find out why you're being persecuted, if in fact you are. Seek to discern if it's because of your Christianity or because of a lack of it. That may not be easy. A friend of mine said, "Just because I'm paranoid, it doesn't mean they aren't after me." It was this same fellow who wanted to join Paranoids Anonymous, but couldn't because the members wouldn't tell him where they met.

J. Allen Petersen of Family Life Crusades uses the illustration of a tea bag dropped into a cup of water. It isn't long before the flavor and color of the tea begins to ooze out of the bag into the cup. What the hot water does, you see, is bring out what's already in the bag.[4] It's something like that with persecution. It can be caused by your right-wise-ness, your being a together person who intimidates the nontogether people around you. If so, accept it. Go on about your business. It goes with the territory. On the other hand, it can be caused by the absence of right-wise-ness in you. If so, you need to deal with that. The hot water situations in life are nothing more or less than occasions which reveal what's really going on inside you.

Which gets us back to the second big word: resourcefulness. In chapter one, I said depression doesn't come to stay, it comes to pass. Like the common cold, it eventually goes away. However, there may be times when it *seems* to come to stay . . . and stay . . . and stay! On those occasions depression must be made to pay dividends! Through resourcefulness you must learn how to get some good out of it. The tragedy is not that we suffer; the tragedy is that we suffer without benefit. As Christians we have the assurance that nothing comes to us which is not first filtered through God's love for us. Therefore, whatever comes to you contains a blessing *if* you can learn to see it.

On my office wall I have an anonymous quotation which reads: "Life consists of endless possibilities cleverly

disguised as seemingly insoluable problems." Every time
I look at that plaque on my wall, I'm reminded that by
being resourceful I can get benefit out of negative
influences and make my trials, such as they are, pay off.

Dr. Boreham of Australia tells of a man who lived in
a comfortable house by a river. Under the house was
a light, airy basement in which he kept a flock of prize
hens. One night the river overflowed its banks, flooded
his basement and drowned his hens. Early the next
morning he was off to his landlord to complain about the
house and give notice of his intention to move.

"But why?" asked the landlord, "I thought you liked the
house."

"I do," said the tenant, "very much, but the river
flooded the basement and all my hens were drowned."

"Oh," said the landlord, "don't move on that account.
Try ducks!"[5] Be resourceful.

E. Stanley Jones once asked an airline pilot if cyclones
can be dangerous to flyers. "You bet," said the pilot, "but
we've learned to use them. You see, they move slowly at
the center and with great speed at the circumference. So
we get on the outer edge and pick up a hundred-mile-an-
hour tail wind. Then coming back we get on the other
edge and gain extra speed going the other way. We use
them coming and going."[6] Be resourceful.

"Brother Stanley" points out that by being resourceful
Jesus took the worst thing that could happen to him,
namely, his death, and made it the best thing that could
happen to you, namely, your redemption. He goes on to
say that's what God wants to do now. He wants to help
you make the worst serve the best.[7]

That will happen when you discover and use the power
in praise. Our prescription says: *Happy are those who are
willing to be vulnerable as part of the cost of experiencing
righteousness (right-wise-ness) — who through praise put a
positive, creative meaning on negative influences and thus
are able to benefit from them.*

"In everything give thanks; for this is God's will for you in Christ Jesus" (1 Thess. 5:18, NASB). You are not told to be thankful *for* everything, but *in* everything. And why? Because an attitude of praise puts you in a frame of mind which enables you to get traction out of trouble—go-power, if you will—and thus to benefit from it.

A mule fell into a dry well. After trying various ways to get him out without success, the owner instructed his boys to bury the poor beast. But the mule refused to be buried. As the boys threw the dirt down on him, the mule simply trampled on the dirt until finally enough dirt had been tossed on him so the plucky old mule just walked right out of his hole! That which was intended to bury him turned into a means of blessing through his resourcefulness. And through praise you can develop the resourcefulness to work your way out of the hole of depression.

A very successful minister shares how early in his ministry he had a terrible experience with depression which lasted for nine months. His spiritual battery was mighty low, but from somewhere deep inside him the Spirit of God beamed forth the message—ever so faintly—"Hang in there, Lee. Hang in there." He writes: "My life was like a lake in a time of drought. Time was when the lake had overflowed, forming a river that blessed cattle and people as it ran through meadows and villages. My life, once, had overflowed with joyous, exciting service. But the emotional reservoir of my life had been used up. There had been more outgo than input and, even as the lake had dried up, so my life felt empty. As an empty lake reveals the muddy bottom, ungainly stumps and slime, so also in me raw, ugly emotions were exposed and reached up to plague and at times control me. I was their prisoner.

"As I rested in my hospital room, I started in a feeble way to believe and (at my doctor's suggestion) to give thanks (for even the smallest things about me, a soft bed, a cup of coffee, a bird's nest just outside my window). As

many people prayed for me, God's healing processes
were at work. True, I *felt* no better. But the lake, as it
were, was filling in again; the ugly emotions and night-
mares were less violent. After months of waiting, the good
feelings returned and with them the zest for work and
service. It was as though the lake were full enough
now to overflow again. The joy of living and loving
had returned."[8]

How did he do it? Through praise! By hanging in there
and by being thankful *"in* everything." Pain without profit
is a bummer! Nobody is the better for it. So don't endure
it. Use it. Through praise develop a positive mental
attitude toward it. Through resourcefulness make it an
instrument of growth—a means of working your way out
of the black hole of depression into the bright light
of reality.

The worst things about you are not the only true things
about you. Let me repeat that: *The worst things about
you are not the only true things about you.* The bleak
things. The grim things. Even the grimy things about you
are not the only true things about you and your situation.
One of the sad side effects of depression is that it makes
you forget every victory you've ever won. Every good
thing you've ever done. Every beautiful thing that has
ever happened to you. But to forget the glad things by
focusing on the bad things is to lose sight of reality.

J. Wallace Hamilton tells about the young son of a
minister, who used to sit in the front pew of the church
while his father preached. In the proscenium arch over
the pulpit there was a row of lights which, to help from
getting bored when his father preached too long, he
named for the books of the Bible: Isaiah, Jeremiah,
Lamentations, Ezekiel, and so on. One day, after church,
this little fellow was quite distressed and his father asked,
"Son, what's troubling you?"

To which the boy replied, "Daddy, Lamentations has
gone out!"

Dr. Hamilton adds: "Well, amen! Let it go. We could do with less lamentation and more laughter in the house of the Lord."[9] I agree, for ours is a joyous faith.

THE THIRD BIG WORD IS REALISM

What I have for you, dear reader, is not good advice! It is good news. The good news that through praise you can become reconciled to reality. By putting a positive, creative meaning on negative influences, you can benefit from them, and, as our prescription concludes: *God's will—your highest good—will come to you in the now.*

As I explained in chapter three, the kingdom of God is the will of God done in your life now—here on earth—as it is being done in heaven. When you organize your life under that single ultimate, you fulfill one of your most basic needs: something to live for. Something truly worthwhile. Something lifelong. Something to which all other goals can be subordinate. And something which is utterly, absolutely, and incontestably reliable.

The only ultimate which meets those specifications is the kingdom of God, that is, the will of God—your highest good—lived out in the now.

When God's will becomes your will, you get unstuck. One cause of depression for a born-again Christian is getting stuck in the present and losing sight of the future. But with the will of God becoming your will, you have both help for today and hope for tomorrow.

Did you ever notice what the Holy Spirit inspired Paul to write in Romans 5:3, 4? Let me quote it for you: ". . . we exult in our tribulations, knowing that tribulation brings about perseverance; and perseverance, proven character; and proven character, hope."

You might wish it were otherwise, but both Scripture and your own life experience make it clear that hope cannot come any earlier in the sequence.[10] Tribulation. Perseverance. Proven character. And *then* hope.

So take heart: "Blessed are those who have been persecuted for the sake of righteousness, for theirs is the kingdom of heaven. Blessed are you when *men* revile you, and persecute you, and say all kinds of evil against you falsely, on account of Me. Rejoice, and be glad, for your reward in heaven is great . . ." (Matt. 5:10-12a— italics mine).

And what is that reward? Not the streets of gold. Or the jasper walls. Or the eternal mansions. Or the gates of pearl. Your reward is nothing less than *God himself.* The glory of his presence. The wonder of his smile. The delight of his commendation: "Well done, good and faithful slave; you were faithful with a few things, I will put you in charge of many things; enter into the joy . . . *the joy . . .* of your master" (Matt. 25:23, NASB).

CORRECT SOUL EROSION

In a superb article entitled *Pulling Out of Depression,*
author Eda LeShan makes this telling statement: "Depression used to be a well-kept secret, but these days a great
many perfectly nice, normal people are acknowledging
that they go through periods of depression. I consider this
a step in the right direction, for there is nothing worse
than feeling depressed and trying to keep it a secret."[1]

I can identify with what she has written, because as
I survey my own gathering courage over the weeks it's
taken to write this book, I can see how I have gained
strength to be open and honest with you. I've shared my
own experience, and that's been risky for me. I want the
affirmation, approval, and love of others. Hopefully, as a
result of my being open and vulnerable, all of us are the
better for it. It is intensely satisfying that many who first
heard this material on a set of teaching cassettes[2] were
freed to disclose and deal with their own battle with
depression.

The fact is we all have "one of those days" from time
to time. Some have many of them. I enjoy the story of
the railroad engineer who crawled out of bed one
morning and stubbed his toe on a chair. While he was

shaving, he cut a hunk out of his upper lip. Half-awake, he reached for the wrong bottle and gargled with Vitalis Hair Tonic. When he opened the garage door, he found a flat tire on his car. He called a taxi, got halfway to the railroad yard and discovered he's left his wallet home with all his money. His imagination did flip-flops thinking of the fun his missus would have with that little windfall. At the crack of dawn he climbed aboard his locomotive and started the day's run through the mountains. Rounding a curve he looked up and saw another train, a quarter mile away on the same track, heading toward him at full throttle. With a heavy sigh the engineer said to his fireman, "Have you ever had one of those days?"

We all have days, sometimes weeks, even longer periods of time when we're victimized by gloom. And as Eda LeShan observes: "In order to cope with depression we need to understand it, acknowledge it, accept it—and allow ourselves to feel it. It has a wide variety of causes, symptoms and degrees of intensity. It can hit suddenly with the ferocity of a tornado and dissipate almost as quickly; it can also grow very slowly and linger quietly for many years. But regardless of when or how or why it comes, it helps to know as much as possible about it."[3]

With the objective of knowing as much as possible about it let me set before you three alternatives. Maybe they'll help you, as they have helped me, to correct soul erosion should it occur. Because that's what neurotic depression is: a complex, multi-faceted, baffling assault on your soul—your mind, emotions, and will—leaving you depleted and less than fully productive. The three alternatives are these: *break down; break out; break through.*[4]

THE FIRST ALTERNATIVE IS A BUMMER

Depression is not a simple disorder. It is not susceptible to simplistic solutions. Left untended, depression can grow increasingly painful. So the first alternative—*break down by reason of neglect*—isn't very appealing, nor are the easy answers some popular speakers and writers put forward. Even what I have suggested in this book is just one way of looking at one phase of depression. Hopefully, there will be some positive spillover which you will find helpful in dealing with other forms of depression. The truth is, however, there is no set formula which, if followed, will help everyone with every form of depression every time.

THE CURE DEPENDS ON THE CAUSE

Dr. Roger Barrett, whose book *Depression—What It Is and What to Do About It* is, in my judgment, a contemporary classic on the subject, says: ". . . if you are depressed because you are failing to live up to your values, or are sinning, then it is quite likely that anti-depressive drugs will only provide temporary relief. Or, if you are excessively dependent and passive, you are not likely to profit from a confession of waywardness. If you are lonely and depressed because your anger and hostility cuts you off from all those who get close to you, you are not likely to benefit from a period of rest or a vacation away. *Despite the similarity of the symptoms of depressed people, they're simply not alike in how they got that way, and it is not likely that everyone will get out of it by doing the same thing*"[5] (italics mine).

A GOOD PLACE TO BEGIN

With that background and a reminder that our primary concern in this book is neurotic depression, one way to start to correct soul erosion is to learn to separate the physical and emotional from the spiritual. You are a tripartite being composed of body, soul, and spirit. If you can distinguish between these three aspects of your personhood, you will be in a better position to pinpoint the true cause of a given mood at a given time and thus get on with the cure.

GET AND KEEP PHYSICALLY FIT

Since all depressions are, to some extent, related to how you're "wired up," it's important to seek medical help. Your family doctor would be the best place to start, and you might discuss with him the wisdom of seeing an endocrinologist. This particular specialty zeros in on what we might call your "control glands"—thyroid, parathyroid, adrenals, etc.—which supply minute amounts of various hormones to your body. Even minuscule differences in hormonal level (a few parts per million) can have a dramatic effect on how you feel.

Psychiatrists, as you know, are medical doctors as well as psychotherapists. What you may not know is that in recent years they have enjoyed excellent results in treating depression through chemotherapy. An article in the *Reader's Digest* explains how chemotherapy works:

"In between each nerve cell in the brain is a little space called a synapsis, which is filled with fluid and activity. A nerve impulse has to cross this gap to get from the end of one nerve to the beginning of the next. And it does this by chemical transmission. The nerves excrete certain substances called biogenic amines (proteins formed in part by amino acids produced in the body) into the synapsis and then reabsorb them. The amines transmit the impulse from one nerve to the next.

"Normally this process goes on continuously. In the depressed person, this doesn't happen. Either the depressed individual doesn't produce enough amines, or the amines are destroyed too rapidly. In other words, there seems to be a deficiency. Two groups of drugs—tricyclic antidepressants and monoamine-oxidase inhibitors—appear to increase the amount of amines available in the synapsis . . . and get that old neuron network moving again."[6]

What's necessary, you see, is to maintain what Harvard psychologist Gerald L. Klerman calls "a particular carburetor mix,"[7] that is, a proper balance between various chemical compounds within your body so mood swings are kept within tolerable limits. So getting and keeping physically fit will help. As a wise old country doctor once told me: "If you let yourself get run down, you'll start thinking the good Lord doesn't love you any more."

YOU'RE VULNERABLE EMOTIONALLY

As Jon Tal Murphree says so cleverly: "Some persons are always feeling of their feelings to feel how their feelings are feeling. They often feel that their feelings are not feeling as good as their feelings were feeling the last time they felt of their feelings to feel how their feelings were feeling. They take their spiritual temperature by their emotional pulse and appraise their relationship with God by the way they feel at the moment. Obviously any person's relationship with God would be pretty precarious if it rested on such tenuous foundations as feelings."[8]

You will always (or at least should always) experience some fluctuation in your feeling tone. It's not only normal but desirable that there be an undulation—an ebb or flow—to your moods. You can't always be on the mountaintop. In fact, there are few more serious heresies in my judgment than the "top of the mountain" myth,[9] the notion that because you are a born-again Christian you will never have any more ups or downs. It will be all ups. That just isn't so!

YOU'RE NOT INVULNERABLE SPIRITUALLY

Some of God's grandest saints have suffered from depression. In fact, as I pointed out in chapter ten, the closer you get to God, the more ups and downs you're likely to experience. It goes with the territory. By just getting closer to him, you become increasingly aware of areas in which you need to grow. That awareness produces struggle. The old nature doesn't want to change. Sometimes it puts up a horrendous fight. And the new nature doesn't always win. As we all know, defeat is a "downer." So hopefully you'll realize your walk with God is going to involve some valleys as well as some mountain peaks, and you'll position yourself to benefit from both.

In my book *Hey! There's Hope!*[10] I've described the typical vacillating nature of the Christian life as we alternate between moments when we're filled with the Spirit and moments when we're carnal. I point out that we are never partly one or the other. It's not both/and. It's a clear-cut case of either/or. I've graphed it out to show we are either dominated by the flesh (carnal) or controlled by the Spirit (Spirit-filled).[11]

The relevancy of *that* to *this* is seen when we overlay (figure 1) your carnal/spiritual graph—showing spiritual lows and highs—with (figure 2) your emotional/physical graph—showing the cyclical nature of those quite normal biochemical undulations all people experience—and (figure 3) your life experience graph—showing the erratic nature of circumstances to which you are subjected with little "everyday" crises interspersed with occasional "moderate" and "major" crises.

If you overlay all three of those graphs (figure 4 is elongated to suggest an indeterminate period of time), you can see how, if an unforeseen circumstance *of the same magnitude* (for the purposes of illustration let's say the "major" kind) puts you into a state of crisis at the same time you're on the down side of your emotion-

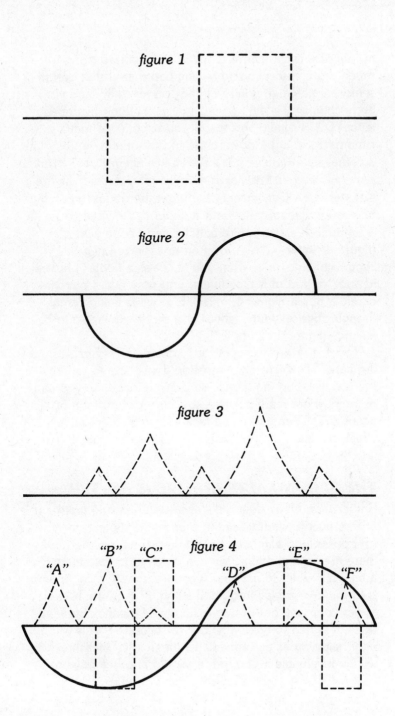

figure 1

figure 2

figure 3

figure 4

"A" "B" "C" "D" "E" "F"

al/physical cycle (figure 4, letter "A"), you're going to be much more susceptible to feeling bad than if that circumstance came when you're hitting "on all eight" and your body chemistry is aiding your mental outlook (figure 4, letter "D"). Equally obvious, if you experience that circumstance and a down cycle at the same time you're in a carnal state, you've got three strikes against you. Your sense of being in crisis almost "goes off the scale" (figure 4, letter "B")! Conversely, if you get the double whammy of a tough circumstance and a down cycle when you're in a Spirit-filled state, you're better able to cope with it (figure 4, letter "C"). And, if an unexpected negative circumstance comes when you're "fit as a fiddle" physically and "on top of it" spiritually, you may ride it out with barely a ripple (figure 4, letter "E"), while being carnal, though physically OK, leaves you more vulnerable to bad feelings (figure 4, letter "F").

You see, the causes of a breakdown are several, as are the cures. To correct soul erosion it will help to separate the physical and emotional from the spiritual, so you can pinpoint more readily the reason for a given mood on a given day. Then you can attack the problem in ways which focus on the real cause, not some imaginary one.

THE SECOND ALTERNATIVE IS BETTER

Rather than *break down*, it's obviously better to *break out* of depression when you're in it or feel it coming on. It isn't possible to eliminate indigo moods all together, but there are several things you can do to moderate them just a bit. "It's easier to *act* your way into right thinking than it is to *think* your way into right acting."[12] And the best way to act your way out of depression is by means of graded tasks designed to build a record of successes. This will not only help you as an immediate "emergency measure," it will be invaluable in the future should another wave of depression hit you. You will have some positive life experiences, some successes you can fall back on.

SIX WAYS TO BREAK OUT OF DEPRESSION

Despite the poverty of easy-answerism, let me suggest six ways you can break out of depression by concentrating on small, short-term gains.

FIRST—GET OUT

Avoid being alone. I'm sure you remember with delight special moments spent alone. Curled up with a book before a crackling fire on a crisp wintry day. Lulled into "letting go" by the gentle motion of a boat on a quiet lake. Relaxed in the solitude of a sandy beach where warm sun and cooling breeze combine to provide a special kind of comfort. But with the onset of depression your need is not to be alone, it is to be with others. Rather than isolation, seek socialization. Get with people. Avoid being alone, because as Dr. William Parker points out: "When we put up a good front of cheerfulness for the sake of others, we actually start breaking out of the downward spiral of emotion."[13]

SECOND—WORK OUT

A lot of evidence is developing showing the linkage between good mental health and physical exercise. *Time* magazine, July 24, 1978, reports "some psychiatrists now routinely prescribe jogging instead of pills for moderate depression. Others use it to break down patient's defenses in talk therapy, and a few believe running produces chemical changes that help cure serious disorders."[14]

Eda LeShan also makes a strong case for physical activity. "I've discovered that I can't overcome my feelings of helplessness and lethargy until I begin to *move*. No matter how tired and despondent I feel, I go for a long walk or swim. At times I'm sure I'll simply sink like a lead weight to the bottom of the pool—but I don't, and I feel better."[15]

If you have a sedentary job with less flexibility in your schedule than someone like Eda LeShan, who is self-employed, you can work out right where you are—at your desk. The following motions designed to work off emotions are condensed from Executive Fitness Newsletter:[16]

1. "After each phone call, before you hang up, squeeze the phone as tightly as possible and then let go. This is a great way for getting rid of muscle tension.

2. "With arms parallel to the floor, clasp your hands in front of your chest and push as hard as possible. That, too, will help relieve tension.

3. "Rest your hands on your desk, feet about 3 to 4 feet away from the desk. Keep your back and arms straight, then slowly do a push-up. Great for tense back, shoulder and chest muscles.

4. "Grasp the bottom of your chair with both hands, keeping your feet on the floor, your arms and back straight, and lift up; you will remain seated, but the tension will go.

5. "Walk! Find an excuse to walk—*anywhere*. Don't sit at your desk for more than an hour without a break, even if it consists of nothing more than marching around your desk a few times.

"Although indoor exercise equipment is ideal, these simple steps will provide the physical outlets for the natural physiological and psychological tension that is part and parcel of your executive office!"

It comes down to this: Your body is God's temple (2 Cor. 6:16). For his sake and yours raise the quality of your "temple maintenance program." *Do* something to take charge of your life situation. Learn to pray what

"Cherry" Parker calls the doers prayer: "Lord, what do
you have for me to *do* today?" Then, as he suggests,
"collect magazines for the hospital, or go down to church
and stuff envelopes—the more mechanical the task, the
better. And if it accomplishes the double purpose of
throwing you in with people, better yet."[17]

THIRD—HELP OUT

Perhaps you're thinking, "Dr. John, how can I be of any
help to anyone when I'm a basket case myself?" Well,
you *can* help. It *will* help. So you *should* help. Nothing
will get you out of that basket quicker than doing something to help someone who's in worse shape than you are.

A world-famous psychiatrist was asked: "What
would you do if you felt you were on the verge of a
breakdown?"

He said, "I would find the poorest, neediest family I
could and spend the day with them. I would clean their
house. Cook their meals. Wash their laundry. Care for
their kids. I'd do anything and everything I could to help
them. In the process I'd be helping myself." So help out.
Helping alters your focus from self to others. It also
alleviates self-pity.

FOURTH—TALK OUT

I almost wrote "cry out," because what I mean is to let it
be known you're having a bout with the blues. Nothing is
worse than being depressed and trying to keep it a secret.
So talk to a counselor. Or a minister. Or an empathetic
friend. And when you pick that person, be sure you pick
a listener, not a lecturer. We can learn a lot from our
heavenly Father in that regard. When Elijah, his servant,
hit the pits after he'd been on the mountaintop overcoming the prophets of Baal, he got so depressed he
wanted to die. When the Lord found him in that state, he

didn't give Elijah a lecture. He gave him a lunch (!) and let him rest. It was after he had eaten and slept that Elijah was able to hear the still, small voice (1 Kings 19:1-12). So take a leaf out of the good Lord's Book. When you're looking for someone to talk to, make sure he or she is a listener, not a lecturer.

FIFTH—MOVE OUT

Seek out people and situations that generate joy. Unfortunately, some people and situations are neurotic themselves and spawn depression. So move out of such relationships and situations whenever you can.

Change the way you talk to yourself. Build a Positive Mental Attitude diary. Record the good thoughts, the good moments, the good things you did throughout the day.

Develop an Alphabet of Affirmations:

"**A**sk, and it shall be given to you" (Matt. 7:7).

"**B**ehold, I stand at the door and knock; if any one hears My voice and opens the door, I will come in to him, and will dine with him, and he with Me" (Rev. 3:20).

"**C**ommit your way to the Lord, trust also in Him, and He will do it" (Psalm 37:5).

"**D**elight yourself in the Lord; and He will give you the desires of your heart" (Psalm 37:4).

And so on with the balance of the alphabet. Commit as many of these affirmations as possible to memory. Invite the Holy Spirit to bring them to mind when things look bleak.

Reward yourself for positive thoughts—*never* for negative thoughts! Argue with yourself, if necessary, but when you win a victory over negative thinking by using your PMA diary or Alphabet of Affirmations, go get a milk shake or a piece of your favorite pie. Reward yourself in some small way for positive thinking. Never let negative thoughts go unchallenged.

Sing. Don't just listen to music. Make music—even if you're off key!

Most important of all, praise the Lord and give thanks. The Bible is full of evidence in support of the power of praise in overcoming depression. So learn to praise the Lord—anyway!

SIXTH—STICK IT OUT

Depression is self-lifting. It doesn't come to stay. It comes to pass. So hang in there. A kindergartner complained of a tummy ache. His teacher sent him to the principal to see if perhaps he should go home. A bit later the boy returned with his back arched forward and his shirt unbuttoned leaving his stomach exposed.

"What on earth are you doing?" the teacher asked.

"The principal told me to do this."

"Tommy, it's bad enough to act like that without lying."

"But, teacher," the lad insisted, "the principal *did* tell me to do this."

"What did he say to you?"

"Well, when I told him my tummy hurt, he said if I could stick it out till noon he'd take me home in his car!"

Get out. Work out. Help out. Talk out. And move out. Then having gotten a better perspective—a new focus on yourself and your situation—stick it out! Remember: "A hero is someone who is brave five minutes longer."

THE THIRD ALTERNATIVE IS BEST

In the beautiful San Joaquin Valley where I live, we sometimes have soil erosion problems—not as serious as in other parts of the country, but a concern nonetheless. The problem occurs when weather and other factors negatively affect the rich earth which produces such abundant crops. Sometimes soil erosion can be so serious it's necessary to completely reorganize the way a piece of land is used to make it productive again.

Similarly, to correct soul erosion you may need to completely reorganize your way of thinking about life. The result—rather than *break down,* or even *break out*—you experience the joy of *break through!* The apostle Paul defines the kingdom of God as "righteousness, peace and *joy* in the Holy Spirit" (Rom. 14:17). Clearly *the* Spirit, God's Spirit, is willing. Are you? What it takes is a decision by you to obey the conditions required to break through. A decision to be filled, that is, controlled, dominated, directed by the Holy Spirit (Eph. 5:18-20), and thus to enter the kingdom of God which is righteousness, peace and *joy.*"

TO SUM IT ALL UP

Our Lord's Beatitude

"Blessed are the poor in spirit, for theirs is the kingdom of heaven" (Matthew 5:3).

Our Adversary's Anti-attitude Perfectionism—The denial of your essential humanity with unrealistic expectations demanding you be *more* than OK, that is, *super*normal.

RX FOR PERFECTIONISM
"Happy are the truly human—who are free to experience all of their feelings, accept their imperfections and give themselves permission to grow. God's will—their highest good—will come to them in the *now.*" (JAL paraphrase)

Joy will come when you know in your heart, as well as your head, that God loves your "bad guy" areas as well as your "good guy" areas—maybe more!

Our Lord's Beatitude	*Our Adversary's Anti-attitude*
"Blessed are those who mourn, for they shall be comforted" (Matthew 5:4).	Worthlessness—Programmed for failure by perfectionism you succumb to chronic regret. The feeling: "Not all good I must be all bad!"

Rx FOR WORTHLESSNESS

"Happy are those who know what it really means to be sorry—who acknowledge the futility of chronic regret and actively employ God's provision (confession, repentance and forgiveness) for failure of all kinds. They will be given the double cure of comfort and courage."
(JAL paraphrase)

To think more highly of yourself than you ought to think is pride. To think less of yourself than you ought to think is false humility. To think soberly (Matt. 5:4; Rom. 12:3) is to think realistically and hence to think mental health.

Our Lord's Beatitude	*Our Adversary's Anti-attitude*
"Blessed are the meek, for they shall inherit the earth" (Matthew 5:5).	Acquisitiveness—The frantic effort to acquire "obvious" evidences of worth: money, success, fame, power, leaving you terribly exposed to loss.

Rx FOR ACQUISITIVENESS

"Happy are those who claim nothing—who recognize over-stress when they see it, abandon the world's way

of determining one's worth and live with eternity's values in view. The whole earth will belong to them."
(JAL paraphrase)

Remember: "It is not he who has little who is poor, but he who wants more!"

Our Lord's Beatitude	*Our Adversary's Anti-attitude*
"Blessed are those who hunger and thirst for righteousness, for they shall be satisfied" (Matthew 5:6).	Hedonism—Your natural need for pleasure to relieve stress becomes perverted. Boredom and dread ensue: "If all *this* won't satisfy, what will?"

Rx FOR HEDONISM
"Happy are those who are hungry and thirsty for righteousness—who, as a life style, deeply desire to please God—the only One worth pleasing. They will naturally, spontaneously and enthusiastically become more and more whole" (JAL paraphrase).

Someone has said: "Satan has all the glitter, but God has all the gold." When Jesus promised you'd be "satisfied," he wasn't talking about providing you with enough soul food to avert death, but with enough to restore a state of normalcy in you. Literally to "fatten you up" spiritually. To make you more and more whole.

Our Lord's Beatitude	*Our Adversary's Anti-attitude*
"Blessed are the merciful, for they shall obtain mercy" (Matthew 5:7).	Defensiveness—Retroflexed anger provokes a brittle attitude toward self and others. Acts of "charity" are largely manipulative, i.e. getting "strokes" for yourself.

Rx FOR DEFENSIVENESS
"Happy are those for whom extending forgiveness
becomes second nature—who are able to love their
neighbor creatively, assertively and redemptively, because
they do so from the perspective of healthy self-love. They
will be given the privilege of being human, too"
(JAL paraphrase).

The phrase Jesus used in Luke 6:37, "pardon, and you
will be pardoned," literally means "release and you will be
released." There are tremendous personal implications in
that for you. You cannot afford the luxury of an
unforgiving spirit. It will make you sick. In the end it will
destroy you. But if you release, you will *be* released! So
let your animosity go. Relinquish your anger and hostility.
Give yourself a reward: the privilege of being human, too!

Our Lord's Beatitude	*Our Adversary's Anti-attitude*
"Blessed are the pure in heart, for they shall see God" (Matthew 5:8).	Fragmentation—Out of touch with your true feelings, accelerating discontent is accompanied by unwillingness/inability to accept responsibility for yourself.

Rx FOR FRAGMENTATION
"Happy are those who are undivided (integrated)—who
are in touch with their feelings, goals, and desires and
accept responsibility for themselves when they are less
than whole. They will know that they know that they
know God accepts them" (JAL paraphrase).

The Lord gives you many gifts, but the first and finest is
the gift of yourself, the knowledge you are acceptable to
him. You didn't choose me, Jesus said, I chose you
(Luke 15:16). Think about that. You have been chosen

and accepted by the good Lord himself. You can't do any better than that!

Our Lord's Beatitude	*Our Adversary's Anti-attitude*
"Blessed are the peace-makers, for they shall be called sons of God" (Matthew 5:9).	Aggression—A dripping source of pathology, you are increasingly isolated as hateful attitudes/behavior alienate you from the objects of your anger.

Rx FOR AGGRESSION

"Happy are those who are always ready to initiate peace—who have the strength to lovingly confront, the willingness to reestablish broken relationships and the maturity to leave the response up to the other guy. They will be recognizably Christian" (JAL paraphrase).

Peace is not the absence of disturbance. It is assurance *in* disturbance. That assurance comes from knowing you're a King's kid. A child of God. Therefore you can respond to aggression from a position of strength.

Our Lord's Beatitude	*Our Adversary's Anti-attitude*
"Blessed are those who are persecuted for righteous-ness' sake, for theirs is the kingdom of heaven" (Matthew 5:10).	Depression—Darkly suspi-cious with only temporary relief via often desperate behavior to prove you're *supernormal.* Inevitable failure ="the pits"!

Rx FOR DEPRESSION

"Happy are those who are willing to be vulnerable as part of the cost of experiencing righteousness (right-wise-ness)—who through praise put a positive, creative meaning on negative influences and thus are able to benefit from them. God's will—their highest good—will come to them in the *now*" (JAL paraphrase).

The happiest Christians I know are those who are willing to take the risks involved with standing up for righteousness (right-wise-ness). These are the people whom Jesus is making whole. When he was here on earth and healed people, he didn't make them all eyes. Or all ears. Or all fingers and toes. Jesus didn't make them *weird*. He made them *whole*. That's what Jesus wants to do for you. He wants to make you whole!

JESUS AND THE BOTTOM LINE

Did you notice as we were going through the Beatitudes how Jesus kept going back to *the* basic of all basics? He started with an invitation to be truly human (Matt. 5:3). But immediately he returned to the bottom line: Be sorry (Matt. 5:4). Guilty, but forgiven—praise the Lord!

Then he suggested certain decisions you need to make if you're going to have a life of joy. Claim nothing (Matt. 5:5). Commit yourself lock, stock, and barrel to righteousness (Matt. 5:6). But ever so quickly he got back to the bottom line again: Be merciful (Matt. 5:7). Let forgiveness become second nature to you.

Then he poses another decision. A variety of voices and values clamor for your attention and allegiance. Reject all which will dilute the quality of your Christian life, he said. Be undivided, solid, integrated (Matt. 5:8). But once again Jesus gets to the bottom line: Be a peacemaker (Matt. 5:9). Be recognizably, tangibly, measurably Christian. *Almost every other Beatitude has to do with the kind of attitudes which will make you happy, healthy and whole: Be sorry. Be merciful. Be a peacemaker. Forgiveness—received and extended—is basic to mental health. It is truly the bottom line!*

Just in case it didn't register the first time around, let me reiterate the difference between a shame-oriented

conscience and a guilt-oriented conscience. The former
feels guilt but is unaware of or unsure of forgiveness.
The latter feels guilt but allows for and is confident of
forgiveness. The difference is monumental! It is the
difference between sickness and health. Between despair
and hope. Between self-rejection and self-acceptance. So
don't miss Jesus' repeated emphasis on "the bottom line."

Finally, he calls you to a decision to be vulnerable for
the sake of righteousness (Matt. 5:10-12). As part of the
price *and prize* of being a put-together person—grounded
and whole—learn to make tribulation work for you and
thus benefit from it.

When all this happens, God hedges you in. He walls
you off, as it were, from will-of-the-wisp moods. By
dealing creatively with neurotic depression, you give the
heavenly Father the conditions he needs to help you build
a better defense against exogenous depression. Though
devastating circumstances may come like a bolt out of the
blue, catch you off guard, and knock you down, they
cannot knock you out (2 Cor. 4:9, Phillips).

THE BENEFITS OF
BREAKING THROUGH TO JESUS

You can't be rejected—because you are fully loved by
the only One whose love means anything in the long run
(Matt. 5:3).

You can't be threatened—because you admit your
failure and know you are accepted (Matt. 5:4).

You can't be cheated—because you claim nothing and
yet enjoy everything (Matt. 5:5).

You can't be defeated—because your goal is righteousness and you *shall* (categorically) be victorious
(Matt. 5:6).

You can't be offended—because you have abandoned
the world's way of measuring one's worth (Matt. 5:7).

You can't be ignored—because extending forgiveness
has become second nature to you and your sincerity will
show through in spite of any slights (Matt. 5:8).

You can't be manipulated—because you are always ready to initiate peace and mature enough to leave the responsibility for response up to the other guy (Matt. 5:9).

You can't be killed—because in the highest and truest sense of the word you're dead already! Dead to yourself. Alive to God (Matt. 5:10).

You may suffer organic or endogenous depression, but even then, by the process of right perspective, you will have put yourself in a position where you can benefit from it. Where you can gain the good God promises to bring "in everything" (Rom. 8:28). Can you imagine anything more wonderful than that? No wonder Paul was moved to say: "Now to Him who is able to do exceeding abundantly beyond all that we ask or think, according to the power that works within us, to Him be the glory in the church and in Christ Jesus to all generations forever and ever. Amen" (Eph. 3:20, 21, NASB).

EPILOGUE

We've come a long way together, you and I. You have my appreciation and admiration for having come this far. Before we part company for a while, allow me a couple of minutes more.

Neurotics are made, not born. Primary "credit" for all neuroses—*and everyone has them*—goes to Satan. But he rarely gets directly involved. He does most of his dirty work through people who themselves are his victims, as were the people he used to trigger neurotic tendencies in them, and so on, and so on, and so on!

I guess none of us will fully grasp the devastating consequences of the fall (Gen. 3) until, in the New Creation (Rev. 21—22), we have a better basis of comparison between God's intention for us and the dreadful effect of Satan's intervention on us. That's why those sections in this book dealing with forgiveness— what I call "the bottom line" in chapter eleven—are especially important.

Even as you are not the culprit but the battlefield, so, too, with the people Satan has used to affect you adversely. They need to be forgiven *almost as much* as you need to forgive them. So do it. OK? OK!

A prayer of praise is also in order. You and I can be genuinely grateful for the remodeling job our loving Lord has done, is doing and will continue to do in us (2 Cor. 5:17; John 3:7, 16; Phil. 1:6; 2:13). In chapter one I wrote of moving toward that level of self-acceptance where you can look in the mirror and say, "God loves you and I do too." Hopefully you're there. So let's wrap up our time together on a note of praise.

"It's good to be reminded neurotics are made not born. It frees me, Father, to be really thankful for the way you made me. For the way I was *born*. Full of innocence. Rich in potential. Truly human.

"What I *am* is ever so much less than what I *was* at birth, and 'credit' for that denigration of your image in me goes to the world, the flesh and the devil.

"But I praise you, Father, for being ready, willing and *able* to remake me in keeping with what you intended me to be in the first place.

"Thank you for Jesus through whom you are restoring the wholesomeness lost through my own wrong choices and sin. Thank you for releasing my full potential. Thank you for helping me regain my true humanity. I want ever so much to cooperate with you in this remodeling process. To do so is my decision of faith, hope, and love. In Jesus' name, amen."

Blessings!
JAL

NOTES

Two. What God Taught Me About Neurotic Depression
1. *Amplified Bible* (Grand Rapids, MI: Zondervan Publishing House, 1965),
   p. 5-New Testament
   Also: A. T. Robertson, *A Grammar of the Greek New Testament in the
   Light of Historical Research,* (Nashville, TN: Broadman Press, 1934),
   p. 39.

Three. It's OK to Be Human
1. Roger Barrett, *Depression* (Elgin, IL: David C. Cook Publishing Co.,
   1977), p. 46.
2. *Eternity,* (June 1971), p. 19.
3. Hannah Whitall Smith, *The Christian's Secret of a Happy Life* (Old
   Tappan, NJ: Fleming H. Revell Co., 1942), p. 26.
4. Dr. M. Roberts Grover, Jr., Director of Medical Education at the University
   of Oregon Medical School. Quoted from a lecture.

Four. Guilty, but Forgiven—PTL!
1. Cecil G. Osborne, *Yokefellows Newsletter* (printed sometime during 1978).
2. Roger Barrett, *Depression,* p. 185.

Five. Get off the Fence
1. For Dr. M. Roberts Grover's cassette and graphic on stress, write to
   University of Oregon, Health Services Center, Portland, OR 97201.
2. Ibid.
3. Refer to *Up the Staircase Backwards,* Lucille Lavender, (Denver, CO:
   Accent Books, 1978).
4. Ralph W. Sockman, *The Higher Happiness* (Nashville, TN: Abingdon
   Press, 1950), p. 68.
5. Ibid., p. 68.
6. Harold Blake Walker, *Power to Manage Yourself* (New York: Harper &
   Brothers Publishers, 1955), p. 97.
7. J. Wallace Hamilton, *Ride the Wild Horses* (Westwood, NJ: Fleming H.
   Revell Co., 1952), p. 59.

Six. Break Out of Boredom
1. A quote of Bernard Iddings Bell in *The Higher Happiness*, Ralph W. Sockman, p. 94.
2. Richard H. Schneider, *Guideposts* (July 1970), p. 29.
3. Ibid., p. 29.
4. Roger Barrett, *Depression*, p. 222.
5. Jon Tal Murphree, *When God Says You're O.K.* (Downers Grove, IL: Inter-Varsity Press, 1975), pp. 44, 45.
6. Ruth Harms Calkin, "Beautiful Fact," *Lord, I Keep Running Back to You* (Wheaton, IL: Tyndale House Publishers, Inc., 1979), p. 18.

Seven. Be Real and Heal
1. Raymond L. Cramer, *The Psychology of Jesus and Mental Health* (Los Angeles, CA: Cowman Publications, Inc., 1959), p. 130.
2. Ibid., pp. 130, 131.
3. From a column by Gene Brown in *Danbury News Times,* Danbury, CT.
4. Roger Barrett, *Depression*, p. 56.
5. *Perfect Marriage*, cassette album (Project Winsome Publishers, P.O. Box 111, Bakersfield, CA 93302).

Eight. Put It All Together
1. Roger Barrett, *Depression*, p. 97ff.
2. From an undated, unnotated clipping which attributes the quote to J. Wallace Hamilton under the heading "Still the Trumpet Sounds."
3. Adapted from: Charles L. Allen, *God's Psychiatry* (Westwood, NJ: Fleming H. Revell Co., 1953), p. 150.

Nine. Retreat from Bitterness
1. Quoted in an article by Wendell W. Price, *Psychology for Living* (October 1978), p. 16.
2. Adapted from an article by Ross Blake, *Pulpit Digest* (July 1960), p. 45.
3. Arthur Digby, "Life Is Relational," *Pulpit Digest* (May 1969), p. 39.
4. Billy Graham, *The Secret of Happiness* (Garden City, NY: Doubleday & Company, Inc., 1955), p. 91.
5. David W. Augsberger, *The Love Fight* (Scottsdale, PA: Harold Press, 1973), p. 1.
6. Ibid., pp. 3-13.

Ten. Hang in There
1. Reference to "a righteous man" is implied by the context when in Job 1:8 Jehovah asks if Satan has considered Job, "a blameless and upright man."
2. A. W. Tozer, "The Editorial Voice," *The Alliance Witness* (March 6, 1963), p. 2.
3. I am indebted to J. Wallace Hamilton for several thoughts included in this chapter, adapted from *Ride the Wild Horses!*
4. Quoted by Morris Sheats, *You Can Be Emotionally Healed* (Fort Worth, TX: Harvest Press, Inc., 1976) p. 66.
5. Quoted in the sermon by J. Wallace Hamilton, *Ride the Wild Horses!* p. 146.
6. Adapted from *The Way*, E. Stanley Jones (Nashville, TN: Abingdon Press, 1946), p. 239.
7. Ibid., p. 239.
8. Lee Whiston, "The Breakdown," *Faith at Work* (March 1978), p. 30.

9. J. Wallace Hamilton, *Horns and Halos in Human Nature* (Westwood, NJ: Fleming H. Revell Co., 1954), p. 154.
10. Roger Barrrett, *Depression,* p. 205.

Eleven. Correct Soul Erosion
1. Eda LeShan, "Pulling Out of a Depression," *Women's Day* (Nov. 20, 1978), p. 50.
2. Cassette album on depression (Project Winsome Publishers, P.O. Box 111, Bakersfield, CA 93302).
3. Eda LeShan, *Women's Day,* p. 52.
4. A. Graham Ikin, "Victory over Suffering," quoted by Gordon Powell in "Release from Guilt and Fear," *Guideposts* (1961), p. 165.
5. Roger Barrett, *Depression,* p. 200 (italics mine).
6. Mackey Brown, "Return from Despair," *Reader's Digest* (August 1978), p. 137.
7. Alice Kosner, "What to Do When You're Really Depressed," *McCall's* (November 1977), p. 281.
8. Jon Tal Murphree, *When God Says You're O.K.,* p. 92.
9. Roger Barrett, *Depression,* p. 135.
10. John Allan Lavender, *Hey! There's Hope!* (Denver, CO: Accent Books, 1978).
11. Ibid., p. 45ff and 124ff.
12. E. Stanley Jones, quoted by Roger Barrett, *Depression,* p. 206.
13. Quoted in "Your Spiritual Workshop," *Guideposts* (May 1969), p. 18.
14. *Time,* (July 24, 1978), p. 42.
15. Eda Le Shan, *Woman's Day,* p. 52.
16. Quoted in a public relations newsletter, *Executive Fitness Newsletter,* published and distributed by Mayflower Movers.
17. "Your Spiritual Workshop," *Guideposts,* p. 19.

Epilogue
1. John Allan Lavender, *Why Prayers Are Unanswered* (Wheaton, IL: Tyndale House Publishers, 1967, 1980); *Your Marriage Needs Three Love Affairs* (Denver, CO: Accent Books, 1978); *Hey! There's Hope!* (Denver, CO: Accent Books, 1978); *Hang Tough in a Hostile World* (Denver, CO: Accent Books, 1978).
   The material in this book is also available as a cassette album (ten cassettes with listening guide) through Project Winsome Publishers, P.O. Box 111, Bakersfield, CA 93302.

BIBLIOGRAPHY

Allen, Charles L. *God's Psychiatry*. Westwood, NJ: Fleming H. Revell Company, 1953.

Barclay, William. *Gospel of Matthew*, Vol. 1. Edinburgh: The Saint Andrew Press, 1956.

Barrett, Roger. *Depression, What It Is and What to Do about It*. Elgin, IL: David C. Cook Publishing Co., 1977.

Cammer, Leonard, M.D. *Up from Depression*. New York: Pocket Books, a division of Simon & Schuster, 1971, Pocket Book edition.

Chappell, Clovis G. *The Sermon on the Mount*. Nashville, TN: Abingdon Press, 1930.

Cramer, Raymond L. *The Psychology of Jesus and Mental Health*. Los Angeles, CA: Cowman Publications, Inc., 1959.

Crowe, Charles M. *Sermons from the Mount*. Nashville, TN: Abingdon Press, 1954.

Ellison, Craig W. *Self Esteem*. Oklahoma City: Southwestern Press, Inc., 1976. Christian Assn. for Psychological Studies, 1976.

Flach, Frederic F., M.D. *The Secret Strength of Depression*. New York: Bantam Books, Inc., 1974.

Graham, Billy. *The Secret of Happiness*. Garden City, NY: Doubleday & Company, Inc., 1955.

Hamilton, J. Wallace. *Horns and Halos in Human Nature*. Westwood, NJ: Fleming H. Revell Company, 1954.

Hamilton, J. Wallace. *Ride the Wild Horses!* Westwood, NJ: Fleming H. Revell Company, 1952.

Heard, Gerald. *The Code of Christ*. New York & London: Harper & Brothers Publishers, 1941.

Hunter, Archibald M. *A Pattern for Life*. Philadelphia, PA: Westminster Press, 1953.

Jones, E. Stanley. *The Way*. Nashville, TN: Abingdon Press, 1946.

Jones, E. Stanley. *The Way to Power and Poise*. New York and Nashville: Abingdon-Cokesbury Press, 1949.

LaHaye, Tim. *How to Win Over Depression*. Grand Rapids, MI: Zondervan Publishing House, 1974.

LaHaye, Tim. *Spirit-Controlled Temperament*. Wheaton, IL: Tyndale House Publishers, 1966.

LaHaye, Tim. *Transformed Temperaments*. Wheaton, IL: Tyndale House Publishers, 1971.

Lampe, G.W.H. Hugh Jones, and P. S. Watson. *What Did Jesus Mean?* London: A. R. Mowbray & Co., Ltd., 1955.

Lloyd-Jones, D. Martyn. *Spiritual Depression*. Grand Rapids, MI: Wm. B. Eerdmans Publishing Co., 1965.

Lowen, Alexander, M.E. *Depression and the Body*. Baltimore, MD: Penquin Books, Inc., 1972.

Martin, Hugh. *The Beatitudes*. New York: Harper & Brothers Publishers, 1953.

Murphree, Jon Tal. *When God Says You're O.K.* Downers Grove, IL: Inter-Varsity Press, 1975.

Pike, James A. *Beyond Anxiety*. New York, London: Charles Scribner's Sons, 1953.

Powell, Gordon. *Happiness Is a Habit*. Carmel, NY: Guideposts Associates, Inc., no date.

Rohrer, Norman & S. Philip Sutherland. *Why Am I Shy?* Minneapolis: Augsburg Publishing House, 1978.

Sheats, Morris. *You Can Be Emotionally Healed*. Fort Worth, TX: Harvest Press, Inc., 1976.

Smith, Hannah Whitall. *The Christian's Secret of a Happy Life*. Old Tappan, NJ: Fleming H. Revell Co., 1942.

Sockman, Ralph W. *The Higher Happiness*. Nashville: Abingdon Press, 1950.

Walker, Harold Blake. *Power to Manage Yourself*. New York: Harper & Brothers Publishers, 1955.